The Hightown Bo

Geoffrey Windham

heart & mind

Brentwood England

Also by Geoffrey Windham

Usual Me,
the rants and ramblings of a psychotherapist

and

How to Find Your Self Without Looking

Geoffrey Windham has asserted the right to be identified as the
Author of this Work in accordance with the
Copyright, Designs and Patents Act 1988

First published by heart & mind 2018

ISBN13- 9781723269486

ISBN10- 1723269484

Front Cover:
Geoffrey in Codnor St, 1950

Contents

It used to be me
walking on the wall,
It used to be me
throwing stones in the water,
It used to be me
falling over and scraping my knees.
Now I'm the one who says,
"Be careful" and "Don't fall",
I'm the one who says,
"No more ice cream" and "Time to go home",
I'm the one who dries the tears,
I'm the one whose heart leaps
when a little hand slips into mine.
I'm the one who knows
that you have a future that I am not a part of.
Love may be proved in the letting go,
But right now I want to hold on.

Dedication

This book is dedicated with love
to Carole
and all those who came before me

and to Heidi, Spencer, Tegan, Kaden and Byron
and all those who are yet to arrive

Preface

This book is a deliberate act on my part to complete parts of my life that have remained slumbering in the background of my mind. The following stories have had a huge effect in the shaping of the kind of person I think I am, my beliefs, hopes, fears, expectations, and assumptions about what it means to be a person.

As I continue to write, further memories make themselves known to me. Some of them are bold and arrive with no prior announcement or conscious invitation. Some of them are more cautious and reveal themselves slowly as if they were emerging from a dark and foggy night. Some never fully show themselves at all, as if shy of the light. They are all my interpretations and they are mine. I would even say they are me.

I have corroborated facts and events with friends and relatives, and in those conversations further memories have been triggered. I have consulted census forms and other documents to check events, dates and liaisons.

I have experienced a great sense of the people I have written about, and although I never met some of them, I feel I know them all a little better. I have thought about what their lives must have been like. They all had their struggles, triumphs and tragedies. They all felt loved and rejected. They too argued about things that seemed so important to them, things now forgotten in the mists of time. Some of them are still here and some appeared for just a little while on this Earth and then vanished, as one day we all will.

As I read over what I have written I can see how prejudiced my memories are. I experience the world through the filter of Geoffreyness. I see the world through Jewish eyes. I hear the world through ears tuned by the Western channels of the 1950s and 60s. I feel the world incarnated in a male body. The people, the streets and the houses, the schools and the shops, the clothes and the music, the smells and the tastes and the sounds, all speak through me. The past is between me and the present. My body may be here but I am an historical event.

My Mum is dying. She is in a hospital bed up North and I am sitting in my office down South, two hundred and fifty miles away. Shouldn't I be there with her, holding her hand, stroking her hair, telling her I love her? But I did that last weekend when I visited. I told her I loved her. I thanked her for being my Mum. I sang to her. I cried. First I asked her not to leave me and then I was able to say it was ok and she should go. It was really a release for me. The lump in my throat was nearly unbearable as it is now. She was mostly unconscious, hardly awake. The doctors have their explanations, the nurses are washing and changing her, but she is not waking up long enough to eat and her sustenance is from a drip. Even this is a gamble between her kidneys failing from lack of water and her heart drowning in it. My Mum is dying and I am helpless, there is nothing I can do.

My mind drifts over memories. Times we spent together, things we did. Why are they not clearer? Why can't I remember more of it? Why does it go by so fast? Why didn't I pay more attention, be there? Was I a good son? Did she know I loved her, did she know how much? Why did I take so much for granted, thinking it would be that way forever?

My brothers and sister have been keeping in contact by phone. They recount her latest condition, what the nurses said, what the doctors pronounce. But I know it is just a matter of time, and her life is nearly over. I have been looking at old photos, Mum and her sister as girls sitting on my grandpa's knee, the teenager at college, so bright and hopeful and bursting with life, the teacher in her class photos, the mother with her children. I hear her sweet voice singing in the house when I was a boy. She sang songs from the 1930s and 40s, the American songbook, that strange combination of Jewish sentimentality and the blues. The music is imprinted in my soul.

It's the weekend and we are going back up North to see her. As my wife, my daughter and I walk to the station in the snow, my mobile rings. It's my brother, my Mum just died. We carry on walking, the suitcase wheels noisy on the pavement. We are silent, tears flow; my breath is visible in the cold air. What do you say? What are you supposed to feel? We catch the train into London, and then the tube, then the Virgin train from Euston to Wigan, change and on to Southport. I look out of the window a lot and sigh. My heart is breaking. I distract myself by thinking of all the times I have travelled between North and South for so many different reasons.

The sweet bitterness of loss is coursing through my veins but the moment I say "I love you", I become vulnerable. I know that the moment I give my trust, the possibility of betrayal is created. Sooner or later I will be parted from everybody and everything I love. Love and suffering are inextricably combined, for the nature of love is that the intensity of its passion is fuelled by the pain of its potential and actual loss. This is the great challenge and burden of relationship.

Chapter One

Codnor Street

My birth certificate states that I was born in the Salvation Army hospital at 15 Mitchell Street, Ancoats, Manchester, on January 7th 1948. In my Mum's baby book, she recorded I was born at 10 minutes to 8pm. At that time, my Mum and Dad, Dennis and Rose Windham, lived with Mum's parents at 172 Elizabeth Street. The era I arrived in was an age of proper austerity and poverty, at least where we lived. It was just after the Second World War, unemployment was high, the country was bankrupt, and many things were still on ration. In March of the same year, we moved to 13 St. James' Road where we lived in upstairs rooms let out by Mrs. Gershon who lived in the downstairs flat. Like everyone else I had an identity card, the under sixteen years' variety. It was meant to be valid until 1964. All governments dream of knowing as much about us as possible.

Our first family house was 3 Codnor Street in Hightown, Cheetham Hill. We moved there in July 1949. It was a typical Coronation Street terrace, no front garden, front door on the street, with a paved yard at the back and a wooden latch door leading into the alley. There was a coal hole at the front and on coal delivery day, the coalmen with their dirty faces and their leather aprons shiny from use, would arrive with their horse and cart and tip bags of coal down the hole into the cellar. The women would always check that no inferior coal was hidden in the bottom of the sacks.

The toilet was in the yard at the back. It was a little brick lean-to with a green, peeling wooden door, a chain for flushing, and a high cistern. A brick had been removed from the inside wall and a candle placed there for light. You had to take matches in with you because left there they would get damp. Newspaper torn into rough squares and strung through the corner hung on the wall for wiping your bottom.

If I had to use the toilet at night, I would sit there and sing at the top of my voice so I could be heard in the house. I'd sing then shout, "Can you hear me Mum?" and my Mum would shout back, "Yes, I can hear you." I'm not sure what this ritual kept away but it lived in the dark between the toilet and the back door.

The winters were really cold. There was no bathroom in our house and we bathed in a tin bath in front of the one coal fire in the kitchen. We had no carpets; it was all cheap and cold lino. I would trace shapes with my finger in the ice that glistened on the inside of my bedroom window. "Shut the door" and "Don't hog the fire" were familiar shouts repeated over and over. Sometimes, if I got the chance, I would stand in front of the fire warming my bottom until the back of my legs went red and blotchy, and then I would turn round to warm the fronts. There was no double glazing, and no central heating, we had never even heard of it.

My earliest memory, from about three years old, is of riding my horsey tricycle in the street. On the other side of the block was a yard where hens were bought and killed in the Jewish ritual way. A woman would pick a live hen from a wooden crate, and hand it to the shochet to kill it by slitting its throat, kosher style. This cost a ha'penny. A further payment was made to the women, who sitting on crates wearing long sacks like pinafores, would pluck the hen for you. The blood would drip onto sawdust on the floor and get mingled with the discarded feathers. I would sit on my horsey tricycle watching all this.

As I grew, I learned that orthodox Jews must only eat animals drained of blood and that Jews in Europe and Russia had been murdered for the crime of kidnapping Christian children and using their blood to bake the traditional unleavened bread called matzos for the festival of Pesach. I would puzzle over why someone would want to believe this.

My parents, each in their own way, had a certain inner robustness that they passed on to me. They were dependable, trustworthy people. My Mum was a down to earth, don't make a fuss, kind of woman. An avid picture goer, she styled her dark brown hair after Rita Hayworth, and often wore floral print dresses. She was pretty with a lovely smile and a wonderful singing voice. When I was a child she had a slim figure but in middle age she was embarrassed about being heavier and wore an old-fashioned corset. She used the word "Nageingliate", the Jewish version of "Let it Be", to describe the way she dealt with the world. On the other hand, although she was very shy, she would stand up for herself or her family if she had to. Their style of parenting was of the time, so I was smacked if I was naughty, although they both mellowed as they grew older.

Dad's attitude to life was a kind of acceptance. It wasn't that he lacked ambition, but he had once lost everything; his family, his status and identity. He had experienced having nothing and being no-one, not theoretically, but at first hand. He knew about the impermanence of life from having survived the random violence and the brutality of being a prisoner in a concentration camp.

As a young man, he was good looking and athletic with thick, black, wavy hair, parted on the left. His nose was slightly sharp and his eyes were heavily lidded. When he hugged me I felt his broad chest, his wide hands and the stubble on his face against my cheek. In his thirties, he put on a lot of weight. With hindsight, I can attribute his relationship with food to his experience of being starved in the camp and the great losses he suffered.

Dad had several jobs working for kosher butchers. This had been the family business in Germany but the job I remember best was him being manager at Rudy's Restaurant. From our house, you turned right onto Waterloo Rd, then right again onto Cheetham Hill Rd, and it was situated in a row of shops opposite the Premier Cinema. Rudy's was a restaurant, deli, and snack bar frequented by the local Jewish community and visiting Jewish actors and entertainers like Max Bygraves. Dad worked long hours into the night for Rudy and his wife. He was not at home much during the day and I was told to play quietly so as not to disturb him. He would shout down from upstairs, "Rosie, Rosie, can't you keep them quiet?" This included my brother, Stephen, who is a couple of years younger than me. I liked tin toy cars for a while that I called "bibbers", and I would line them up on the floor and race them. This meant pushing each one to see how far it could go and then declaring a winner. It was difficult to be quiet.

I visited Rudy's when I was five and met Peter the Polish chef. He had one gold tooth which fascinated me and he showed it off with different smiles, posing this way and that. The place was empty and Dad lifted me up onto a wooden chair with a red plastic seat at a formica top table. Peter brought in a slice of melon decorated with a glace cherry. He put it on the table with a flourish and was most disappointed when I didn't eat it because it was too cold.

Dad told us a story about Rudy's concerning the film actor Alfred Marks. He was a regular and one time came in complaining of a bad back. Dad also had a bad back and would use a product called Fiery Jack to ease the pain. He lent it to Alfred but whoever rubbed it in used far too much. Marks half ran, half fell down the stairs, like a mad octopus, clutching his back, swearing and screaming in agony. He hurtled out of the front door never to visit the premises again.

Dad worked there from 1952 and, when Rudy died, Dad was supposed to take over but there was some issue over money with Rudy's wife and family and the deal never went through. There was some schadenfreude in our family when the restaurant closed not long after. Anyway, Dad wanted to be his own boss and with money lent by my Grandparents he bought Joe Max's kosher butcher shop in Southport.

Dad had acquired an old banger which we would have to get out and push if a hill was very steep. We would go on Sunday afternoon drives into the Lancashire countryside with a picnic, sometimes down the East Lancs Road to Southport, which is how they came up with the idea to live there. Mum, Stephen, and I moved there in October 1954 while Dad stayed on in Manchester to work out his notice with Schatz the butcher.

When I was three, Auntie Lily, my Grandma's sister, left her husband to be, a Mr. Henderson, who was never referred to by first name, and my Mum and Dad offered her a place to stay for several months. This was very controversial as the rest of the family did not speak to her because Mr. Henderson was not Jewish. It was called "marrying out". Worse than that for me, she took my bedroom. I was always annoyed with her about this theft, as I saw it. I can't remember moving back as I must have done when she went back to him. Maybe my outrage was the strongest emotion.

We played out in the street and the mothers took turns to watch us. I remember a boy called Sholom, who these days would be classed as "special needs", and how we never played with him. Whenever he appeared the cry would go up, "Sholom's here!" and we would run away. He would spit at us as we ran, and he could spit a long way. How cruel we were, how frightened we really were of him. We played on the bomb sites, and I especially remember bonfire nights held there. I can still see the bonfire's flickering shadows on the rubble of the bombed-out buildings, the sparks floating up into the dark sky and feel the cold November winds on my face cooling the heat of the fire.

Once I noticed two older boys sitting on the kerb a little further down from our house. I went over and sat down next to them with my feet in the gutter. They were playing with a little length of a silver ball chain, maybe six inches long. I hadn't seen anything like it and asked them what it was. They told me it was magic and shook it about, waving it in front of me. I said, "What's magic?" and they told me that if you said a special magic word it would turn into a little magic snake. I said, "Go on then," but they refused saying I wasn't old enough.

How I wanted them to say their magic word and turn the little chain into a snake, but they wouldn't and I went home disappointed. I told Mum but she told me not to be so silly. I think this sparked my lifelong interest in magic, both the entertainment and the shamanistic kind. When I was a little older I would buy magic tricks with my pocket money and bore everybody by asking them to, "Just look at this" over and over.

One of my favourite outings was to the swimming baths at Sunlight House in Quay Street off Deansgate. It was built in 1932 and it was the tallest building in Manchester at the time. Auntie Vivi, my Mum's sister, would take me and my cousin Michael. Sometimes Stephen would come too. It was a magical place to me. The pool was in the basement and there were pillars in the water that held up the floor above. I remember the pool as being an oval shape and I loved swimming around the columns and hearing the water swishing against them.

There were three floors and looking up I could see a tunnel shape rising above me and the moving shadows cast on the wall. On the second floor was a cafe with a brass rail around it and after swimming, with hair still damp, we would sit at a table near the edge and look over at the water below. I can still taste the hot buttered crumpets we always ate there. The pool is still there but these days it is part of a health club owned by Bannatynes.

In Manchester, Monday was always washing day, and the housewives would wash clothes and bedding by hand and then get the water out by putting them through a mangle. I was expected to help by turning the handle, which was hard work. The clothes came through flat and creased and sometimes they had to be put through several times.

Another weekly ritual was donkey-stoning the front step. The housewives could be seen on their knees scrubbing away with their donkey-stones, so-called for the imprint of a donkey on their surface. The stone was the size and shape of a large bar of soap. It was applied wet, and as the residue dried it became a sort of red colour which was then buffed up.

I remember Mum getting her stones from the rag-and-bone man in exchange for old clothes. The alternative was a goldfish in a jam jar and we got one once or twice but they didn't last long. He would come round with a cart, shouting "Ragbo", all one word. I don't know if they ever did get any actual bones, but I suppose they were used for making glue. They sold the rags on to rag merchants, a business in which many of my great Grandparents and older relatives, who had fled the pogroms in Eastern Europe, made their living. The Jews were tailors, cap makers, machinists, and rag merchants. The lowest job was shmeering, which was oiling cloth. It later came to mean something like spreading cream cheese on a bagel

When I was four, I had a hernia operation in Booth Hall Hospital. I was there for three or four days. I remember being in the operating theatre and a rubber mask being placed on my face, and being told to think of Mickey Mouse as the anaesthetic took hold. In those days parents could not stay over but I don't recall pining for them. Stephen had the same operation twice, one on his second birthday May 7th 1952, when we were in hospital together, and later in 1955. Stephen reminded me that the nurses told my Mum that he had refused to eat the dinners because they were not kosher, and she was very proud of that. I had my adenoids removed in July 1952 only a few months later. I went in supposedly to have my tonsils out, which was all the rage then, but they only did my adenoids. I felt a bit cheated.

My other hospital visit was the result of an accident which caused quite a row between Mum and Dad. Dad was out working and I was home with Mum. I was still in nappies but on that day, because I had some kind of gastric flu, I was wandering around with no nappy on. Mum had boiled the kettle on the stove and for some reason decided to put it next to the fire in the fireplace, maybe to keep it warm. Anyway, I sat on the hot kettle. She took me to the Jewish Hospital on Elizabeth Street, but she didn't leave a note about where she was or what had happened. Dad came home, the house was empty, and no dinner had been made. He rushed around to my Grandparents', we didn't have a phone. We were not there and fearing the worst Dad and Grandpa ran up the road to the Jewish Hospital where they found us.

As you can imagine it provoked a huge argument between them all, as to why she had let it happen, and why she hadn't left a note. I had no permanent damage to my bottom, but it became one of those family stories that all families have, and for a while would be brought up. Mum's usual way to deal with Dad's anger was to give him the "silent treatment", something I often witnessed in later years. This could go on for days until he gave in.

My love for football is deeply engrained, and I played in the back yard for hours, either kicking the ball against the wall again and again, or playing reds against blues, depending on which direction I was kicking the ball. So it was natural that when I was four, Dad began to take me to Old Trafford to watch Manchester United and then to the other Lancashire first division grounds, Blackpool, Burnley, Bolton Wanderers, and Blackburn Rovers; all the Bs, plus Manchester City and Preston North End. When we parked at an away game, which was usually in a street of back-to-back houses near the ground, scruffy looking boys would come up and say, "Look after your car mister?" It was a protection racket but we always paid a few shillings.

I saw the pre-Munich Manchester United team play although my memories are a bit hazy. I just have a glimpse of David Pegg on the left wing, one of the players who died in the plane crash. I do remember the strong smell of liniment when the teams ran out, and the surge of excitement in the crowd, singing songs I didn't understand then. Young boys like me would be picked up and passed over the heads of the crowd, by men in their flat caps and gabardine raincoats, over the white painted, round topped wall and onto the side of the pitch where we sat so we could see. It was early crowd surfing.

Dad always took two apples and loose hazel nuts in his pocket for half time. He never queued for pies at the break because they weren't kosher. He had mixed standards, and these became a part of my life. Like all Jews, he "pick and mixed" the rules of Judaism that he lived by. I could not really understand why he kept anything at all or seemed to believe in God.

In the early days we just turned up at Old Trafford and bought a ticket, but later my Dad was friendly with a man called Hymie Mehlman. He was some kind of wholesaler in Manchester and a friend of Matt Busby, the legendary United manager. On match days we would wait near the players' entrance, and then Hymie would appear and ask my Dad how many tickets, and give my cheek a pinch. A few minutes later he would re-appear with the tickets. He was selling them on behalf of the players. They didn't make as much money as they do now. He wasn't totally dependable and sometimes never showed up, so we had to buy tickets from a tout, but my Dad knew most of them and got preferential rates.

When I was about sixteen, Dad, Stephen and I went to Old Trafford to see United play Liverpool. We didn't have tickets and even the touts had none. We went to the players' entrance and Dad asked someone at the door to tell Hymie that Dennis was there. A few minutes later he appeared. He said he had no tickets but that he could take Dad in with him, but not the boys. They went in and Stephen and I walked to a local Seamen's mission where we drank coke and looked at our watches.

The area was pretty rough then and the room we sat in was dark and depressing. With about thirty minutes to go the end of the game, we walked back to the ground. After a while the back gates opened and we went in and watched the last fifteen minutes; they don't do that anymore.

I was nine when I became aware that something bad had happened to Dad. It was Friday night and we were sitting at the table with the Shabbos candles burning bright and a silver goblet of kosher red wine on the white table cloth. I was refusing to eat the chicken soup my mother had served and the atmosphere was tense. Dad began to cry. He said, "I was in a place where you would be glad to have a piece of bread to last all day", and he ran out. I didn't know what this meant but my heart was fluttering. I ate the soup; it was the only thing to do.

As time went by I discovered in bits and pieces that there had been a war, and something called the Holocaust, with places called concentration camps with names like Auschwitz and Belsen, horrible sounding names where unspeakable things had happened, where Jews had been starved and tortured and burned. I learned that Dad's father, mother and brother had been murdered in Auschwitz, as well as many of his extended family, my family. I learned that Dad had been in a concentration camp and escaped somehow. I resisted reading about the Holocaust for a long time but as I grew older I could no longer look away.

For the most part, I have learned to limit myself, especially with pictures of the camps and ghettos and other anti-Semitic acts by local civilians and police across 1930s and 1940s Europe, because I find them difficult to undo once I have seen them. Now when I hear of someone being murdered, I realise, that not so long ago, my family were murdered just for being Jews. Years later I attended a therapy group for "second generation" Jews whose parents had survived. Some survivors spoke at length about their experiences and some little. Dad spoke little but he told different fragments of his experiences to each of us. He never talked about having survived when his parents and brother had died. Unsurprisingly. I also heard how some survivors had gone on to be terrible and abusive parents passing on their pain to the next generation.

It was now that something fell into place for me, something that I had known but not thought about, that my friends had two sets of Grandparents. It was like a mystery that became solved, a peripheral puzzle that I had never really questioned.

I was in my teens before another of these unthoughts became apparent to me. It was in the sixties in Southport, when I was part of a loose group of Jewish teenagers that went out together to house parties, dances and clubs. There grew a habit of parodying our parents, making fun of them, mimicking their habits and ways of speaking. When they did this about my Dad, my friends put on a heavy German-Jewish accent.

On first hearing this it took me aback but I brushed it off as an aberration by those taking him off, but later that evening when I went home, I listened to Dad with newly opened ears and discovered he did have that accent. How could I have missed that all these years? Familiarity I suppose. Not really listening or taking notice of him? Maybe. It also fitted in with Dad having two names. In public, in the shop, he was Dennis Windham, at home to my Mum, he was Hans, that was his "real name"; Hans Windmüller.

To complicate things further, he had, like all Jews, a Jewish name, Yitzchok ben Gedalyah, Isaac, the son of Gedalyah. My Jewish name is the reverse, Gedalyah ben Yitzchok. On the end was Halevi, meaning we were Levites and could trace our ancestry back to Temple times in Israel when the Levites were the servants of the priest class.

The funeral is in the Jewish part of the cemetery in Duke Street in Southport. Her coffin is already in the little brick building known as the "Ohel". The family is there as well as some old familiar faces. They shake my hand and say, "I wish you long life" the traditional greeting at these occasions. At the service I am told I can say the "Kadish" in the Ohel and by the grave but I cannot make a speech or say anything publically about her because of some rule about the time of year. I am reminded why I have had enough of religion. After a short service we all follow the coffin and I watch it being lowered into the freshly dug grave. My brothers and I say Kaddish again. I throw some earth I brought back with me from Israel into the grave. I share it with others. I am numb. I feel the tears in my throat but they won't come out. I look at my Dad's grave next to hers and at others around. I recognize most of the names. A silent community lies buried here.

I reflect on my own life and I know that however much I train I will never run the 100 meters in less than 10 seconds. However much I study physics, I will never mathematically understand the theory of relativity. However much I meditate, I will never win enlightenment. I am already all I can be. The rest is just the desire to consume, be it for financial gain, power, or spiritual progress.

In the land of desire, the objects of my desire have me. In the land of enough, I can see the dance of the void in a stick; I can hear the soundless love songs of the divine in a frog's croak; I can feel the pulse of the universe in my wrist.

Chapter Two

Elizabeth Street

As both my parents worked, I spent a lot of time at my Grandparents, David and Celia Samuels, who lived round the corner from us at 172 Elizabeth Street. They were married in 1921. David told my brother Stephen they were so "feared" of Eli, my Grandpa's father, that they got a rabbi to marry them in secret, at midnight, with two passers-by for witnesses. They both decided on this course of action because David's parents, together with the boss of the sweat shop in Bolton where David was working, had made a shidach (arranged marriage) with the boss's daughter.

In the meantime David had met Celia and they fell in love. After the wedding they continued to live at home and didn't tell anyone they were married for two weeks. I don't know what happened when they did tell. I do know that Grandpa had a bad temper himself, and that my Grandma nearly left him on several occasions.

The house had a few steps up to the front door, which led to a long dark hall. On the left was the work room, then the best room, and finally the kitchen with its stove and table and a fireplace at the far end. There was a scratchy garden at the back and a cellar. Sticky, curly, fly papers that had gone yellow hung from the ceiling, sometimes with a dead fly or two on them.

Grandpa was a tailor and worked from home, making suits for both men and women. The women's suits were called costumes. He made the jacket of the men's suits, which he called a coat. The trousers were made by a trouser hand. A customer would come to the house to be measured and discuss the suit, then a few weeks later return for a "try on", and finally for the completed garment. Grandpa would sit crossed legged on the table when he was sewing and could thread a needle in an instant with his tongue.

Years later when I saw Audrey Horne on Twin Peaks knotting cherry stems with her tongue I thought, "My Grandpa could do that!"

He was a tough, old fashioned man, of about 5' 5", but a softy inside. His hair was combed straight back. He never learned to drive and never owned a car or a house. He smoked Senior Service, untipped. All the kids played a game with empty cigarette packets and we collected ours from him and Dad who smoked Woodbines. We would flatten then flick them, and the one whose card went furthest won them all. It wasn't until years later that I realised a woodbine was a flower.

In the First World War, Grandpa was in the Lancashire Fusiliers, soldier 40257, from December 11th 1915, when he was eighteen. He was mostly a private but was a lance corporal in May 1918 when he was deemed no longer fit for war service because of "injury abroad". He was regularly demoted for getting into fights with other soldiers, mostly over anti-Semitic remarks. Stephen has two of his Great War medals. My Dad's father, Grandpa Gustav, fought on the German side. My two Grandpas fighting each other for King and Country demonstrates to me the stupidity of war and nationalism.

Grandpa David was very sporty and played a lot of rugby and cricket. Part of his competitive character was to make up for his lack of height. He was an active member of the local British Legion, and the first live stage-show I ever saw was with him at their Christmas do. I remember seeing a chorus line of girls high kicking and being strangely excited by it.

He was a great gambler, as were many Jewish men of his generation. He loved to bet on the horses and every day the Sporting Times was delivered at lunchtime. He called it "The One O' Clock." He would stop work when it arrived and study form, the going, the jockeys, and once he had made his decision he would go to the bookies to put his bet on.

In those days betting was illegal except on course. You could put your bet on with a runner who would come round to you, but he preferred going to the bookies himself. I would often go with him until an event occurred which led to Grandma banning him from ever taking me again.

To get to the bookies we had to walk down back alleys with many twists and turns, crossing gutters and drains, skirting parked bikes, and go past peeling wooden back doors and piles of rubbish, until we came to a whitewashed wall with several men, in raincoats and hats, hanging about. We brushed past them into the inner sanctum full of noise and cigarette smoke and just as Grandpa got to the front of the queue a loud alarm bell began to ring and everyone stopped for a moment then dashed for the exit. He grabbed my hand and we ran down the alleys as fast as we could until we got back home.

I found it all very exciting running together, hand in hand, but Grandma was not happy. The bell was a warning that the police were about to raid the place. There was an arrangement between the bookies and the police, no doubt with money involved, that every now and then there would be a raid, and two men were paid to stay and be arrested and fined and then the bookies would open up again.

Grandpa would tell me tales of when he was in a Jewish gang that would fight the fascist black shirts in the streets of Manchester; proper toe-to-toe punch ups. It was before the war in the 1930s, when Oswald Mosley's fascist party held meetings and paraded in Manchester, including Cheetham. Grandpa was very proud he had made a stand.

He always wore short sleeved shirts, even in the coldest of winters, and I can see him now drawing round the brown paper patterns with his triangular tailor's chalk with a circle motif in the middle, and then cutting through the cloth with his huge, sharp scissors. I can see him sewing the white basting stitches that he let me remove sometimes, using a little white tool three inches long with a pointed end and three circular grooves around the handle. He had a proper iron, not electric but heated on an electric stand with three open elements that glowed red.

I remember him using a wooden tool called a klomper. It's a brick-shaped solid piece of wood, with a wonderful patina, flat and shiny on the bottom with grooves down each side that fitted his hand. He used it as part of the ironing process, banging it onto a dampened shmattie placed over parts of the jacket. When he used the iron I loved watching the steam rising and the hiss as the hot metal touched the wet cloth. The klomper was passed down to me, and when I hold it I can feel his hand in mine.

They had a button-hole hand called Alf, who worked at a sewing machine in the window. Grandma would take the trousers out to the trouser hand and then go back to pick them up so I never met him. She would hurry down the street with several pairs of unmade trousers on her arm, sometimes late at night.

An outing for me would be to accompany her to a local shop to purchase supplies, "The Hightown Trimming Stores" which had everything a tailor would need. It was a long shop with many windows and inside it was full of glass fronted wooden drawers up to the ceiling.

Grandma was a formidable woman, quite a beauty in her youth, as Grandpa always reminded everyone, although she had put on a lot of weight as she got older, but I loved being cuddled in her big arms and bosom. She had long ginger hair in her middle age which she would braid at night before going to bed. She had false teeth because as a girl all her teeth had been taken out to save problems later, not uncommon in those days.

I remember her always wearing a full pinny. Her fingers were toughened by years of sewing, and she would show me a gruesome trick of pushing a needle through the skin at the end of her fore finger and not drawing blood.

She was quite superstitious and if she sewed a button on my shirt while I was wearing it, I had to chew a piece of red cotton. Grandma believed in a kind of fate called "beshert", a lucky happenstance, so if you left late to go somewhere and missed a car accident because of that, it was beshert. It also means meeting your soul mate.

Her other big superstition, passed on to Mum, was to say "Kane-en-hori". If someone was talking and mentioned a family member doing well or how healthy there were, any kind of blessing, saying it was a magical ward against the luck turning bad. The actual Yiddish phrase is "Kein Ayin Hora", literally "No Evil Eye". She often hummed to herself as she was doing things and she sometimes sang a strange song which I have not been able to track down anywhere.

"There's a bobby round the corner,
With a number on his coat,
If he sees anybody fighting,
He'll take them by the throat,
And march them down to Strangeways,
And give them fourteen days,
Fourteen days hard labour,
For pulling the donkey's tail.

I work at the railway station,
I do a decent job,
I carry bricks and mortar,
My wage is eighteen bob,
I never miss a quarter,
I get up like a man,
Harum scarum tiddle eye arum
Paddy the Irishman".

Sometimes she would sing, "Solly the Jewish man". "Strangeways" was the name of the local prison.

Thursday was fish day, and Grandma would make chopped and fried fish and boiled gefilte fish with a slice of carrot on top. It was a whole morning's job, chopping the hake and haddock by hand, and then adding matzo meal, onion, salt and pepper. The fish cakes were shaped not round as usual, but formed in the shape of the palm of her hand. When we moved to Southport, she would send us a fish parcel on the train. It included enough fish for all of us, a jam jar of her home made chopped herring, a news letter, and any sewing she had done for Mum.

She packed it all up in a cardboard box, tied it with string, then took it by bus to Victoria station and put it on the guard's van herself, she knew all the guards. When I was seventeen and had passed my driving test, I took over the collecting job from Mum and I would drive onto Southport station platform to meet the 5.30pm and the guard would give me the parcel. Later my brothers Stephen and Paul took over. When we ate the fish for tea it was still warm. I have never tasted chopped and fried, or chopped herring like it. How I wish I could have some now.

She also made her own chopped liver with schmaltz, which is rendered chicken fat and always used chicken livers. To make schmaltz she would slowly fry chicken skin and any bits of chicken fat and drain off the golden liquid. Then she continued to fry the skin and curled up fat with chopped onion until it became really crisp. These little brown crispy bites are gribenis, pronounced "gri-ber-neez".

Grandma made chicken soup the traditional way with an old boiling fowl, its neck, feet and pupak (stomach). She boiled it for about three hours with a carrot or two and a stick of celery and seasoning. When the soup begins to boil, a scum forms on top which she skimmed off with a large metal spoon. We called this "shepping". How often I have watched my Grandma and my Mum doing this. Wonderful with the soup were the little, yellow, unlaid eggs, called eyerlech, dropped in the boiling soup just for a moment. When I bit into them they would burst and fill my mouth with liquid deliciousness. I often burned myself eating them too hot.

Another treat was helzel stuffing. Helzel is the skin of a hen or chicken's neck, stuffed with a mixture of schmaltz, chopped onion, matzoh meal, beaten egg, and seasoning. One end of the skin was sewn up with cotton, and then the stuffing pushed in, not too full as it expands when cooked, and then the open end was sewn up. It can be boiled in chicken soup, but my favourite was when it was roasted in the pan with the chicken. The skin would crisp up and the inside was soft and sensual.

We would have schmaltz butties with picklemeat, vorsht or a vienna, but even on its own, schmaltz spread on a slice of challa is a wonderful treat. I do not allow myself to eat it in these health conscious days. Schmaltz came to mean over-sentimentality or over the top sincerity.

A strange dish was kez and smetana, we called it smetny. If I told you that it's cream cheese and sour cream that would be a poor description, but in a way that's what it is. I never really considered that pouring sour cream over cheese and eating it from a bowl was strange because it was there, and so ordinary, but also because it was delicious and so why question it?

Food was an important part of our lives. It wasn't a substitute for love, but it was love in action. The cook got "nachas" from people enjoying the dish and would want to know that theirs really was the best tsimmes or chicken soup or the moistest honey cake.

When Grandpa died of a heart attack in 1969, Grandma continued to send fish for a while and then it got too much for her and we told her to stop. I only realise now how hard that must have been for her and the loss involved. I thought we were doing her a favour but we were not. We were taking away part of her purpose.

In the 1950s, Grandma kept a couple of hens in the cellar, a throwback to the war years when eggs were scarce. The cellar back door was left open in the daytime so the hens could scratch around in the garden. Coal was also kept in the cellar and sometimes it was my job to fill the coal scuttle in the morning to light the fire, an important task in the winter. This meant me taking the coal scuttle, opening the door to the cellar, charging down the wooden stairs, filling the scuttle as fast as I could, charging back up the stairs and slamming the door behind me, safe from the hens this time. I was convinced that if I spent too long down there, the hens would get me.

Cheetham Hill was a community and all the Jews knew each other. Jewishness was something in the air; a way of being that was not imposed but expressed in everyday life. It was in the streets and the homes and the yontefs, the festivals. It was in the shops. There was the deli "Titanic's" on Waterloo Road, opened by Titanic survivor Joseph Hyman, Margolis the grocers, Malkin's the chemist, and all the kosher butchers. In the delis you could dip your hand into giant tins of pickled cucumbers both sour and sweet and sour, and into the wooden barrels of schmaltz and salt herrings. Butter was loose, weighed on scales and wrapped in greaseproof paper.

The bakers, Needoff's, Tobias, and Bookbinder's sold all the familiar Jewish breads, large and small tin loaves, black breads with shiny cracked crusts, pilots, turbans and challas, pletzels and knots, bulkas, and bagels. We said challa not cholla and bagels not beigels like the Londoners. I loved the honey cake, kichels, and the wine slices which were always different as they were made out of whatever cakes were left over, compressed and soaked in kosher red wine.

At one end of Elizabeth Street was the Marlborough Cinema which later became the Astor Bingo Hall. It started out as the Pankhurst Hall named after the famous Manchester Suffragette family. At the other end, round the corner, was Klapisch the grocer, and Grandma would send me or Stephen on errands there although we were so young.

One shop that really stays with me was the Maypole which smelled like no other shop. The floor was black and white chequered lino, and in the middle was a much handled pole. The Maypole chain was famous for its margarine but for me it was the cheeses. Oh the cheeses and the smell of them. I can smell them now. I think all Maypole shops smelled the same.

When I stayed with my Grandparents, I slept in the front bedroom because for some reason they slept in the back. To the left of 172, on the corner, was the Waterloo Hotel, derelict now, and at 10.30 when it closed, I would hear people on the street outside, speaking loudly, sometimes laughing and singing, sometimes shouting in a strange way. Their voices echoed and their footsteps clicked in the night air as if the pavements bounced the sound upwards. This was an alien world for me; I didn't know they had been drinking. When I asked I was told with a dismissive wave, "Take no notice, they're just shikkeras."

My Grandparents slept on large feather pillows that had been brought over from Russia in the late 1800s. Feather pillows seemed to have been important to the Jews of that era and I always thought they called them peronies, but the word is peronas. Now I believe that this refers to something like an eiderdown. In the

Russian pogroms one of the ways of terrorising the Jews, as well as murder, rape and theft, was to tear open their bedding, and the streets of the shtetl would be filled with feathers. Some argue it was a sexual humiliation.

In the early fifties, they bought the first TV in the family. It was brown and had a 7" screen. There was only the BBC in black and white, and we would watch it sitting cinema style with the curtains drawn. The set had to warm up and we would cheer when the picture finally appeared. When it was turned off the little white dot seemed to last for ages even when the plug was pulled out. My favourite programme was Muffin the Mule. I even went to see Annette Mills, Muffin's puppeteer.

I was part of the first generation to be entranced by TV. We went to the pictures, but that was a big screen in a theatre and involved going out. Watching TV at home on a small screen was more intimate. ITV was first broadcast in 1955 and American shows became all the rage. We watched the Lone Ranger (Hi Ho Silver Away!), and of course Davy Crocket. I pestered my Mum until she gave in and bought me a "coonskin hat". It was called a "fad" and every kid hankered after one. Then the BBC hit back with Robin Hood starring Richard Green. I can still sing those theme songs now.

Every day at 11 o'clock was coffee time and it was my job to go into Grandpa's workroom, take him by the hand and lead him down the corridor into the kitchen for his coffee. This was made by dissolving instant coffee into a saucepan of milk and then simmering it. It was accompanied by hot doorstep toast and butter.

One day I decided to try smoking. All the other men did it. I stole one of Grandpa's Senior Service and a few matches and locked myself in the toilet. I didn't know about inhaling so I just stuck the cigarette in my mouth and tried to set light to the end. I even blew to try to get it going, but no luck. Eventually I gave up, threw the cigarette in the toilet, pulled the chain and went downstairs.

Soon enough Grandpa confronted me. I denied everything until he took me to the toilet and showed me the burned cigarette swimming in the toilet pan. I didn't know cigarettes don't flush. It was the first time I had to bow my head to the inevitable.

They had a big, fat cat called Blackie, who would follow Grandma around almost like a dog, even going walks with her to the shops. Stephen reminded me that on fish day Grandma would boil up fish heads and put them out for Blackie at the side of the house because of the smell. Then she had to keep guard to make sure the neighbourhood cats didn't bully Blackie and eat the fish heads because Blackie was a bit of a nebbish (wimp).

Across Elizabeth Street at 163 was Rydell Mount Shul and behind it was a playing field where Dad played football sometimes. It was a strange pitch, not grass but cinder. There are two occasions I remember well. The first was watching my second cousin Bernard Altman, who is six years older than me, playing football. I was standing on the touchline with his father, my Uncle Joe who was married to Edie, Grandma's sister. Edie and Joe met in a raincoat factory where they both worked as machinists. My Grandma worked on the machine next to Joe and they would jostle each other as she was left handed and he was right handed.

Joe shouted, "Give it to Bernard" the entire match. I felt a lot of affection for him although others found his behaviour irritating. These days I imagine he might be diagnosed as autistic. I was also friendly with Ruth, Bernard's younger sister, and when we moved to Southport she would visit with her parents and we would go walking on the beach, sharing little private jokes and laughing.

I saw her recently at a family wedding and she remembered the last time she visited and expected me to be there for our usual time, but was told by my Mum that I was out with my girlfriend, Carole, who was to become my wife. Well that's the lure of erotic teenage love, it wins every time. Joe had a sister called Betty, and Betty's daughter, Eunice, was born in the same hospital as me on nearly the same date.

The second occasion I remember is watching a football match there on my own and being called a "kike" by an older boy. I didn't know what it meant but I knew it was an insult. I was maybe six. I ran home crying and told my Grandparents what had happened. Grandpa couldn't believe I was crying and even worse that I hadn't punched the other boy. It was the first time I disappointed him. Grandma defending me made it worse. As the eldest grandson I should have been tougher.

In 1956, my Grandparents visited New York to see the Samuels family. They went on the Queen Mary, which had the blue riband for the fastest Atlantic crossing. They stayed there for several weeks, mostly with Grandpa's brother, Lazer. By then we had moved to Southport. My parents wanted to welcome them home, so we drove to Manchester and waited for them in Elizabeth Street. Mum and Dad had bought them a new TV, to replace the old one, and set it up ready.

We waited and waited and it got later and later. There were no mobile phones or internet in those days so we had no idea where there were or even if they had docked. They arrived really late that night and we had a long, tiring drive home. They bought Lone Ranger outfits back for Stephen and Paul, which was a mask, a shiny black embroidered top and a black hat. I can't remember what I got.

I miss our nightly phone calls. At the end they became more of a "Goodnight" than a conversation but it was contact. Even now a thought arises to call her with some news. Then I remember.

It's time for the stone setting, a ceremony to place her gravestone. It's back to Southport again, back to the graveyard, back to the same people that I never see from one year to the next. I know they are sincere, they all know the pain of loss, but now we only have the distant past and our Jewishness in common. After a short service we go to the shul and down into the Bes Hamedrish beneath the main building. This time I am allowed to speak.

"All our Mums are important to us, and I am no exception. There is a great lack of love in the world right now and my Mum taught me the importance of family and how to love each other. She taught by example and I miss her more than words can say".

Attachment, detachment, which is more desirable? In the spiritual world, attachment to the human or non human world seems to be judged as an impediment to freedom. Not at all, it is the evidence for my freedom. I love those I love and I feel loved by them. To denigrate the truth of this is to be an extremist and to miss the humanity of others and the suchness of the world.

Chapter Three

Ancestors and Relatives

I vaguely remember Grandma's mother, who we called Bobbi. Her name was Rebecca Weinstein nee Glass born in 1872 in Kovno, Lithuania. Bobbi didn't speak much English. She was small, wore dark clothes and cooked on an open fire. I loved tasting her home-made raisin wine which she gave me with a jam butty. One of her legs had been amputated because of what they called "Sugar", which I now realise was diabetes.

Bobbi married Chaim (Hyman), a rag dealer, in 1896. He was born in Riga in 1873 and died in 1922. By the time I knew her, Bobbi lived alone in 80 Herbert Street, east from my Grandparents, off Elizabeth Street. In the 1911 census, Chaim and Rebecca are listed with their five children, my Grandma Celia, Lily, Phil, Motti, who became a cabinet maker and emigrated to Australia, Sam, and a lodger. Edie was born later.

Although the family was called Weinstein in England, this was not their original name as they were given names on arrival at immigration, a common practice. Unfortunately, those who knew the Polish name have all gone, and there is no-one left to ask. Some of the same family were re-named Krell as they entered the U.K.

Phil and his first wife had a daughter, named Cynthia, who died from diphtheria when she was seventeen. He later married Fanny and eventually they lived in the flat over our butcher shop in Bold Street. Sam was a journeyman tailor. His wife, Rae Classic, owned the sweet shop, Classic's, with her brother, Julius (Yuddle), on Herbert Street near Bobbi's. Yuddle wore a big, black medical boot. We would go there sometimes and get free samples over and above the ration.

Poland was counted as Russia in those days. It was part of what was known as the Pale of Settlement in Western Russia. Jews were allowed to live there but under harsh restrictions. This did not save them from regular harassment, paying double taxes, and murderous pogroms.

Life became worse after 1881 when the Tsar Alexander II was assassinated and one of the conspirators was a young Jewish woman. So, like countless Jews down the centuries, they moved on again. Most moved to the United States but by the late 1890s about 150,000, including my ancestors, had settled in the UK. Many of them were poor and unskilled.

The British media whipped up racist feelings against immigrants, especially Jews, and an organisation called "The British Brothers League" campaigned against "The scum of Europe" being allowed into the UK. Their slogan was "England for the English" and they held large meetings in the East End of London. One meeting was chaired by Major Evans-Gordon, the M.P. for Stepney, at the People's Palace in Mile End. Several thousand people attended.

"The Aliens Act" was first proposed by the Tory government, but passed by the Liberals in 1905. It controlled immigration and restricted entry for "destitute foreigners", meaning Jews, from Eastern Europe. It was the forerunner of further immigration restrictions.

Jews had been unwanted in England before. They were expelled in 1290 by Edward I after years of being persecuted and attacked. Christians were not allowed to lend money for profit so the job was taken by the Jews and they were hated for it. On death their assets were taken by the crown. Unlike the rest of the population they were not included in any of the rights of the Magna Carta and special clauses mentioned money lending and Jews. In 1218, Jews had to wear a yellow marking badge.

Other European countries had similar clothing requirements, even special hats. Jews were taxed differently and could not own land. The Nazis were not the first.

Grandpa's parents were Samuel Eli Samuel and Rose Sugarman, Mum was named after her. Eli was born in 1874 to Lejzer Zamul and Mera Gittel Festenstein in Marijampole on the Lithuanian Polish border, listed in the census as "Russia Poland". My Mum called him Zaidi. In the 1891 census in Leeds, he was described as a tailor's machinist.

Jacob, Eli's older brother, was an "interpreter reader", born 1856, also listed as "Russia Poland". In the 1901 census, Jacob's job was a synagogue reader and I remember my Grandparents referring to frum (religious) Uncle Jacob in Leeds, inferring he was too orthodox for them. By 1911, he was a mohel (circumciser) and a shochet (kosher slaughterer), a very deadly combination if you ask me.

Grandpa's siblings were Lazer, Elli, Goldie, Anna, Dolly, and Esther. All except Grandpa emigrated to America. Even his father went in 1934 with Esther. They were held back at Ellis Island as Eli was ill but eventually released into Lazer's care. He survived another four years.

My Great Grandma Rose's parents were Nathan Sugarman and Ada Gertrude Michelovsky born in Kalvarijas, Russia. Nathan was a picture dealer. The 1901 census listed Nathan and Ada with their four children, and Eli and Rose with their five children, plus two boarders, fifteen people living in one house.

Rose was killed aged forty five, on the 18th March 1920 by a "lurry". One newspaper report said,

"She had alighted from a tram-car and was running behind in an endeavour to reach the opposite pavement when a heavy motor-lurry passed over both her legs and she was conveyed to the Salford Royal Hospital."

She died later the same day. Another newspaper reported the accident was in Chapel Street, Salford and the inquest gave her address as Woodlands Terrace, Broughton. I can't imagine the effect on the family. Even years later, no-one ever spoke about her to me or mentioned her in my presence. It wasn't done to show those kinds of feelings.

Rose was able to read and write in English. She helped those who were not literate, and could only speak Yiddish. At some point the family changed their name from Samuel to Samuels which was a great secret for some reason.

In the summer of 1968, when I was twenty, I visited New York and met some of the Samuels family. I stayed with my Great Aunt Bubbles (Rose), Goldie's daughter, and her husband, Maurice Shuell, who made cassocks and other religious clothing for the Catholic clergy. Maurice was the first person I met who had a proper flat-top haircut and chewed gum all the time. He embraced the American lifestyle completely.

I knew Bubbles and her daughter, Sandra, in Manchester before they emigrated. Sandra had very bad infantile eczema and my memories are of her being wrapped in bandages and not being able to play.

Maurice met me at the airport, and then took me to their house on Long Island. It was newly decorated in Jewish rococo style. The sofa and armchairs were covered in thick plastic. They had made a special welcome meal in my honour, cabbage stuffed with mincemeat which is my very least favourite; diplomatically I ate it all, hiding my gagging. They were very nice to me though. I was nineteen and it was the sixties, and I was from the North West of England, near Liverpool, and I thought I was cool. I took my guitar with me which I had recently learned to play. They took me out to dinner and it was the first time I had ever encountered a maitre d' and queued behind a fancy rope.

Much more interesting was the visit to Maurice's business. Before we went, he made me promise not to mention us being Jewish to anyone for fear of it harming his business. The factory was downtown under one of the overhead train lines, so pretty noisy. The streets were full of sweaty men rushing around, some pushing clothes on long rails, some just hanging around. Cars were honking and trains rattled above. In his shop window were dummies dressed in catholic outfits for the clergy. Inside, in the steamy back room, was a giant, sweaty, black man with enormous muscley arms, operating a huge steam press. I suspect he did most of the work. After our visit, we had pastrami on rye with pickles and a soda in a local deli.

I enjoyed walking round the city in the heat, and one afternoon I passed a line of queuing people. I asked them what was going on and one man said it was the line for the Tonight show. I stood at the end and eventually we were led into a studio. I had my guitar with me and I felt very proud when Johnny Carson pointed to me and said, "I see we have the hippies in tonight." When I got back to Long island I told everybody and we watched the recording on TV and there I was in the audience. It was the first time I saw colour TV.

One night, Sandy and her friends took me out to a club in Greenwich Village. It was down some rickety stairs and so dark that we were led to our table by a girl with a flashlight. We ordered drinks and sat sipping them with my eyes getting used to the lack of light. Then the band started playing and I thought my drink had been spiked because of the weird visuals I was having, but it was a strobe light, something else I hadn't seen before.

Meeting Great Uncle Lazer was daunting. He had become a very successful surgeon and was quite rich. Like Grandpa, he was a gambler and took me to the racetrack in his brand new open top sports car with air conditioning, which he drove very slowly. We didn't stay long. As a gambler, he didn't like his routine changing. He was in his seventies, but still acting as if he was young. He wore a gaudy short-sleeved sports shirt which he made a point of telling me was silk. His silver hair was oiled and combed straight back. He was short and stocky like Grandpa.

I always suspected some feelings between them. Grandpa had left school early to work as a machinist, so never had the opportunity for the education that Lazer had. Lazer was the golden boy and was fêted as a surgeon. I also met his son, Peter, who gave me my first daiquiri and played me modern jazz on his hi-fi. I was amazed at the sound. I was like the country bumpkin and it seemed that they were not interested in spending much time with me.

One day I was in Central Park playing my guitar under a tree. The park was full of young men my age. Some looked sad and some were being over enthusiastic in the intense way they were throwing footballs to each other. Several of them sat with me and listened to my songs. We got talking and they told me that they were conscripted soldiers waiting to be shipped out to Vietnam. They were smoking lots of marijuana, but the police were nowhere to be seen. I wonder if the boys I met so briefly survived, and if they did how they were affected by it. Another thing I will never know.

Bubbles took me to visit her sister, Shirley, who liked to be known as Vivi like my auntie. It was a two hour drive to the trailer park where she lived alone. Bubbles left me to stay overnight. It was a large trailer but she was obviously the poor relation. Bubbles had set it up on the way telling me how strange Shirley was and how she was bad at relationships. Shirley had married but they were no longer together. She was sweet and made me a lovely dinner and then painted my portrait in oils which I still have. We chatted about life while she painted. It's not a very good painting but it reminds me of her. It hung in my Mum's house until she died.

When my Mum was pregnant with me, there were anti-Jewish riots in Cheetham Hill over the August bank holiday of 1947, and many Jewish shops were attacked. It was in the lead up to the creation of Israel in 1948, and British soldiers were being shot at and blown up in Palestine by the Zionist terrorist gangs; at least that's how they were portrayed in the British press that summer. They considered themselves to be freedom fighters.

The papers headlined the retaliation murder in July 1947 of two British sergeants in Palestine by Irgun, one of the extreme groups, with front page pictures of the soldiers hanging from two trees. British Jews were accused of not being British enough and even though it was so soon after the Holocaust, there was still much anti-Semitism in British society. Jews were thought to be money grabbing and black marketeers. They were the usual easy target in times of austerity, poverty, unemployment and rationing.

One of my strangest jobs as a boy was taking the accumulator to be charged. There were no electrical sockets on the wall in my Grandparents' house, and they would plug things into a two way adaptor in the light sockets, one side for a bulb and the other for an electrical appliance. For some reason people did not do this with their radio, their main source of entertainment, and they had a battery called an accumulator. It was heavy and shaped like a large brick, made of thick glass with a wire carrying handle on top. You could see the acid sloshing about inside.

It was my weekly job to take it to the local shop on Waterloo Road to have it charged and collect the one they had charged up for us. If you held it on your clothes it didn't burn them, but left a white deposit. Imagine giving a young boy that job now.

I was always interested in people's behaviour even when I was little and didn't know the word behaviour except when it was mine and bad. An example is when I was about seven, I shamed my Uncle Bernard. He and my Auntie Vivi, like many couples in those days, went to the pictures regularly. We never said movies. Vivi was the one who was in control of the relationship, often by passive aggression.

They were at my grandparents' house, all dressed up and arguing about what film to see that evening. All the family was there. They continued arguing as they got up to leave. Bernard said, "But I don't want to see that film". In my best adult voice and mimicking my Mum who had said it to me recently, I said, "Well you'll just have to lump it then!" The room went silent. Bernard got the total hump and stormed out. Vivi brought him back and I was made to apologise to him. I didn't consider his feelings and maybe that's why I was punished, but I think I broke the code that all families have about who is allowed to tell the truth. I only said what everyone was thinking.

When I became a psychotherapist I was paid for making observations. Of course, that was with the client's permission and I certainly didn't have Bernard's.

The winter fogs were awful. Day became night as the sunlight was blocked out. The fogs were called "pea soupers" because they had a greenish tinge. Traffic crawled along and people hurried to get indoors holding hankies over their mouths. You could taste the fog, cold and sort of sooty. When you blew your nose your hankie had long trails of black snot on it. People died in the really bad ones. Add to that the fumes you inhaled from open coal fires and the passive smoking endured from most adults, like my Dad, especially on car journeys. He would light up a woodbine and cough and cough and the car would fill up with smoke.

I remember a day's outing to Southport turning into a marathon as we crept home through the fog, with our headlights bouncing back off the yellow-green darkness, and an hour's journey becoming three or four. It was pollution inside and out. The fogs went on well into the sixties and even now air pollution is still killing us.

Mum always maintained that out of all of us I knew Dad best because I worked with him for seventeen years. My judgement is that my best was not enough; I could have known him so much more, so much more deeply, so much more intimately. I never really knew him as a man because I was not yet a man myself. My love was immature rather than conditional.

I question if there is such a thing as unconditional love. I am told this is the best kind, the gourmet version. I think most of us feel in deficit with love, and it is in short supply when we try to find it in the habitual, usual way, acting from the position that I call "usual me".

Coming from this position, nothing is ever enough and love is no different. If, in usual me style, we try to apply some plan, to find a prescription with the goal of feeling more loved and giving more love, whether it be by the practice of new kinder behaviours or some meditation technique or the application of compassion, it comes from not enough, is an expression of dissatisfaction, and it is just fiddling with the contents, redecorating, moving the furniture around, polishing and cleaning what already exists, trying to update tradition, always searching and re-searching for more. It is up to each one of us to create love now with no reason or evidence to back it up.

Chapter Four

Yiddishkeit

I was Jewish and felt a kinship that was wordless. The people were characters, it was as if they had not been homogenised. Refugees and children of refugees have lived a life of adventure, even if bad, and have been moulded by hardship, their lives or ways of life have been threatened and their ways of being and stories reflect that. They have been touched by the impersonal and that touch is like the forerunner of death's touch. The brushes with death that we survive do something to the way we perceive the world, to the way we perceive ourselves. It's like Peter the chef showing off with his gold tooth. It wasn't really showing off for me; he was demonstrating both to the world and to himself that he was still alive, still him.

I knew a man who had been sent to England by his parents to escape the pogroms when he was nine, and he had walked alone across Europe from Poland and then got a boat to England. He never saw his parents again and yet he wasn't bitter. He was bearing his burden with grace. He had managed to love again.

There were the outward Jewish signs like eating kosher and going to shul but it was just what you did, and I felt special, not better but special. So special I didn't realise how poor we were or that we lived in what would now be called a slum.

There are two main types of Jews, Ashkenazi and Sephardi. Ashkenazi Jews come mostly from Germany and Eastern Europe, and Sephardi mainly from Spain and Portugal. Some of the customs are different. Even though my Dad was from Germany he was Sephardi, so when we went to shul it was to the Spanish and Portuguese.

There was and is a religious hierarchy of Jews. Some keep nothing. There are the ordinary ones like my family who ate kosher and kept fleishich and milchich, (the separation of meat and milk), but would travel in a car on Shabbos and didn't cover their heads except in shul. Some of the ordinary Jews would keep kosher at home but eat treif (not kosher) out. Some would eat out, but not meat or chicken. Then there were those who were more frum (religious). The men tended to have a beard and would cover their heads all the time. They would never eat out. Some of them as well as the ultra orthodox would not do any work on Shabbos and would employ a "Shabbos goy", a non-Jew, to come in and do things for them, like turning lights on and off, or lighting a fire.

The real frummies, the ultra orthodox, are now known as Charedi. Both men and women have a very strict uniform code. The men wear long black silky coats with a belt and big furry hats, and unlike us, who wore our tzitzis in; they have their tzitzis hanging out of their shirts. Tzitzis are the fringes on a kind of under-vest, a little prayer shawl. It comes from a Biblical command. They wear beards and long payers (the hair in front of the top of the ears). They tend to look very pale and the young boys look very similar. The women wear head scarves and sheitals (wigs) and long skirts. They have lots of children as contraception is forbidden and they want large families anyway. The young men are often Yeshiva Bochers, which means they go to a yeshiva (religious school), and study Torah and Mishna and Gemmorah all day. They don't just go to shul only on Shabbos like my family and they pray three times every day. They often speak in Yiddish which I don't understand. Yiddish words are part of my vocabulary, but not as a whole language, and my Dad would not speak German at home. I understand why, but it would have been nice to be bi-lingual.

Another division was where you originally came from, where "the haim" (home) was. The main Ashkenazi ones were the Litvaks, Lithuanians, the Polaks, Poles, and the Yekkes, German. There was some rivalry between them, sometimes even as far as not inter-marrying. The divisions were not discrete and there was overlapping.

Shul or shool is the Jewish word for synagogue. Synagogue is rarely used by one Jew to another Jew. It is a word used by non Jews or by Jews to non Jews. There are other Yiddish words usually reserved for Jewish ears only like Yidden Fient for anti-Semite. Then there are abusive words to describe non-Jews like Goy, Yok, Yachel (said Yaykel), and Baitz for men and Shicksa for women. There are, of course, plenty of abusive words for Jews.

There was a large Sephardi shul on Cheetham Hill Road, but Dad and I went to a small front room shtiebl. My first spiritual experience was in that little room. It was Friday night and my Dad took me to my first Friday night service. There was a lot of standing up and sitting down, lots of singing and amens, but the part that really made a huge impact on me was when I was ushered by the shammas from my seat up a few wooden steps onto the bimah (reading platform) in the centre of the room. It was surrounded on all sides by men. I was the only boy there.

The Friday night service is a joyous welcome to Shabbos as if Shabbos were a bride being brought in to her wedding. The room was mostly lit by flickering candles. I stood there on the bimah, with my little kepple on my head, not knowing what to do or what was expected of me. This was the part of the ceremony where the chazzan sanctifies wine in a silver goblet, holding it up and singing a blessing. Then the goblet was touched to my lips and I had a little sip of the sweet red wine.

At that moment heaven opened up for me, the candle light shimmered with magical, dreamlike, supernatural quality, the wine was like nectar, and the songs being sung were as if the angels were singing. I was in the presence of God. Of course these were not my words at the time but this is how it has stayed with me, a description evolving over time even until now as I write these words.

Yontefs were especially enjoyable time. The real Hebrew word for festival is Yomtov, but I heard and said Yontef. The best one was Pesach, in English, Passover. The first two nights were called Seder nights. This was a big family feast with prayers, the telling of the Jews escape from slavery in Egypt, and the singing of songs. Grandpa led the reading from the Haggadah, the special book of Pesach. There are illustrated children's versions. I still have my first adult one, signed by me, "G Windham 1959", its pages stained with red kosher wine. It is bound in brown leather and has a metal inset on the front cover, a picture of Jerusalem.

Grandpa had little education so he could not read much Hebrew and he muttered most of the reading but nobody ever mentioned it. There was me and Stephen, Grandpa and Grandma, Mum and Dad, Auntie Vivi, my Mum's younger sister, her husband Bernard Finlay (Nathan Finkelstein), who was a vet, and my cousin Michael. Sometimes other relatives joined us, and later my brother Paul.

We all crowded into the middle room, and sat round the table, decorated with a large goblet of wine for Elijah the Prophet's visit. At some point in the evening one of the kids would open the front door to let him in. One of the adults would shake the table from underneath so the wine in the goblet moved and they would swear it was Elijah. There was the Seder plate with three pieces of matzoh in a silken bag, charoses, (a sweet paste mixture of chopped apple, chopped nuts, wine and cinnamon), a lamb shankbone, karpas (parsley, greens or chervil), maror (bitter herbs, horseradish), a bowl of salt water and a burnt egg still in its shell. We had a little ceremony of tasting each, except the egg which was never eaten. They were all symbolic of something to remind us of the past. For example the salt water was to remind us of the tears the Jews wept. Charoses, signifying the mortar the Jews used in their work, was my favourite.

We got through the prayers, the grace before meals, and then the grace after meals, as quickly as we could. I always liked the fir kashes or four questions, called Ma Nishtana, asked out loud by the youngest, with prescribed answers about the meaning of Pesach. The meal had the most courses of any meal apart from the "breaking the fast" feast at the end of Yom Kippur, the Day of Atonement, when we had sponge cake and tea to begin.

At Pesach, we started with Grandma's chopped and fried fish with tomatoes and chrain (horseradish and beetroot sauce), and chopped herring on matzoh, then chicken soup with her alkis (dumplings), also known as kneidlach, then chopped liver on matzoh, followed by a braised steak and roast chicken course with potatoes and vegetables and then fruit. Our family rarely made puddings or desserts.

When the meal and the boring prayers were over we got to the communal songs; Adir Hu, Dayenu, Ki Lo Noeh, Hodu, Echod Mi Yodea, L'Shona Haba'ah and my favourite, Chad Gadyo. As I got older I learned them off by heart and was even able to keep up with my Mum and her sister, my Auntie Vivi who would sing Chad Gadyo as fast as they could, side by side, their faces flushed. It was a joyous time. At the end of the evening, the kids "hunted" for the afikoman, which is a small piece of matzoh that is hidden and whichever child found it was promised a prize. I don't remember there ever being one, but it didn't matter. Once Grandpa had a raisin stuck to his glasses and hadn't noticed, and I remember us all really laughing and laughing. He took it well though.

Yom Kippur, the Day of Atonement, when we are supposed to reflect on our behaviour and make amends for wrongs committed against God and other people, is very different. The fast, no food or drink, lasts from sunset to sunset the next day. It begins with an evening service in shul called Kol Nidra, a very solemn affair. I was captivated by the music, especially the haunting melody of the Kol Nidra prayer. The songs are so sentimental, so sad, and so Eastern. Many of the world's religious songs have similar musical structures and scales in common, as well as the way people sway as they pray, we call it davening.

There is no requirement for a boy under thirteen to fast but by the time I was seven I was determined to do it. I remember sitting in the kitchen at my Grandma's, with my belly rumbling, determined not to give in, when my cousin Ruth came round and ate something. Grandma said "See, you should eat something too!" So after not much internal struggle I agreed and had an apple and a cup of tea. I felt like a failure for a while but it soon passed.

Hanukka, the Festival of Lights, was always enjoyable, again because of the songs that we sang together, especially Ma'oz Tzur, and the ceremony of lighting candles on the menorah each night. It was not a High Holiday like Yom Kippur and Pesach so working was allowed. We also got little presents, sometimes a small amount of money called Hanukka geld. These days with the unstoppable march of consumerism and with the dates of Christmas and Hanukka being close, the presents have become much more lavish. Later, when I found out about Christmas, as an outsider not caught up in the madness, I got a sense of the tawdry nature of what Christmas had become even in the fifties and sixties.

My next best Yontef was Purim which celebrated the saving of the Jews in ancient Persia from a plot to kill them by Haman, vizier to King Ahasueras. A Jewish girl called Esther has become Queen but the King does not know she is Jewish. Esther is an orphan and has been adopted by her cousin Mordechai who Haman hates. Mordechai finds out about the plot. After some complications, Ruth reveals her true religion to the King, the Jews are saved and the baddies are killed. The story is read out in shul from the Megillah or Book of Esther. Like many Bible stories, it's a bloodthirsty tale but as a boy I didn't mind that at all.

During the reading in shul, we had rattles that we would shake, as well as boo and stamp our feet, every time Haman's name was mentioned. It was a tradition but the shammas never liked it, and would shout at the kids to keep quiet. Shuls can be very noisy and chaotic.

The food associated with Purim is called homontaschen (Haman's pockets). They are triangular cakes made with a sweet filling made of mohn (poppy seeds), butter, milk, sugar, honey and beaten eggs. The front is left open so you can see inside. Some people dress up at Purim, either as a character from the story or as some other Jewish celebrity.

The focus of a lot of our festivals is remembrance. Sometimes in prayer, sometimes in the telling of stories and sometimes with symbols. One of the messages of remembering the Holocaust is so that it will never happen again. There are similar messages about other great human tragedies, but I think that all this remembering doesn't really help much as the evidence is that is does happen again and keeps on happening.

In my work as a psychotherapist, I facilitate clients in the telling of their story, in feeling really heard and known. To be free is to be able to move beyond the story, to stop being sorry for ourselves, to stop identifying ourselves as victims or victors, to be free to live here and move towards a future that is not a mirror image of the past.

Much of the remembering we do as individuals, families, cultures, religions, and nations, is indulging, is about being right, about winning and losing. This is how we let the power holders control us. One of the struggles of my life, has been to recognise the rich heritage I have been describing and at the same time to let it be in the past. The wars waging around us are a product of indulging in and continuing the past. It has become a point of principle for me. It's time that we all healed our broken hearts.

Mum loved children, which was why she loved being an infant teacher, but she was inward looking towards her own family all her life. Family was all important to her. About two years after my brother Stephen was born she got pregnant again. She went full term, in fact over the date that the baby was supposed to be born and, later she told me she felt there was something wrong, but that nobody would listen to her. The baby, a girl, was born dead with the umbilical cord wrapped around her neck.

As a four year old, I knew nothing of this. I assume after two boys she would have wanted a girl. I remember staying at my Grandparents and sleeping over more than usual and that was ok, but I don't remember any outward signs of grief, although I suppose I may have blocked it out. As far as I know she didn't try for another baby until 1955 when we lived in Southport. Paul was born in 1956.

In Jewish law a baby that dies as young as my sister is not named or given their own grave. They are buried within a few days with an adult who has recently died. The baby was buried in Failsworth Cemetery in Manchester on the 24th of October 1953. Shiva, the seven days of ritual mourning and prayers are not observed. In my fifties, and feeling sad about this, I decided to name her Alice, after my Dad's stepmother, Elsa/Elise. I felt it important that she had a name. How Mum and Dad dealt with their grief I do not know.

I started school in January 1953 at the Wilton Polygon, which became known as King David. It was the first modern school I attended and had a playground that wasn't all paved. There were some grassy areas with swings and other play equipment, and it wasn't surrounded by a high brick wall. The classrooms were light and airy and the desks were new, not from the 1930s. The headmistress was a Miss Vitofski who had been the head of the Temple school in Cheetham Hill. I remember her as fussy and intense with quick movements and quite thin.

Both Mum and Auntie Vivi taught there and although I was in Vivi's class, I was never in Mum's. Mum being a teacher there sometimes made it difficult for me, and I never felt fully accepted, not just by the kids, but also by the teachers. I seem to have garnered a reputation for being something of a trouble maker and other kids would often tell on me even for things I hadn't done.

The most famous family story that Mum loved to tell concerned me "flooding" the school. I do remember the incident but more with frustration than anything else. We had just finished an art lesson and the art teacher had left me and a few other children to clear up and gone on a break. The job I got was to wash out all the jam jars in the sink. We had just been using them and they were full of murky looking paint water that had been dipped in a lot. I lined up all the jars next to the sink, which was wide rather than deep, and turned the cold water tap on. What happened next was that the top of the tap came off in my hand and a stream of water shot up into the air. I couldn't stop it or get the top of the tap back on. Soaking wet, I ran to the staff room where I knew the teacher would be, and knocked on the door. After what seemed like ages the door opened a crack and one of the teachers looked out.

"Oh it's you, come back later",

and the door closed.

I knocked again louder, and eventually the door opened again.

"I told you once, come back in five minutes!"

and the door closed.

I hesitated, what to do? I paced up and down. I knocked again.

"What?"

"Sorry, but the tap came off and the water came out, and I can't get it back on, and I don't know what to do."

This time the message was heard, but at least 10 minutes had gone by. They rushed to the classroom with me running behind. The sink had overflowed, and the water had come under the classroom door into the corridor. The school was evacuated and we all had to line up in the playground while the water was pumped out and they made sure there was no danger of electrocution. Well it wasn't my fault!

When I picture Mum's grave I always see Dad's next to hers. I think of his life. We all have a burden to bear but his burden seems harsh. I cannot imagine my parents and brother being murdered and being able to laugh again, but he did. I wish I had told him how much I admired his strength to carry on living and not just surviving, but I was too wrapped up in my own life to consider such ideas at the time.

Carole and I decided recently that we should book and pay for our funerals and buy a burial plot. We visited a green burial site in a bluebell wood quite close to us and decided to be buried there. I chose a banana leaf coffin. When we were filling in the forms, the salesman asked us for our religion. We looked at each other and said we had none. This was a real wrench for me. In my dislike and criticism of all religions, being born Jewish still holds a powerful sway over me and although I do not practise any form of Judaism I still think of myself as Jewish and not being buried in a Jewish cemetery is a big deal for me. I rationalise it by telling myself it would be hypocritical to be buried in a religious way.

I tell myself how lucky I have been to have a warm bed at night and friends and family, special ones to love who love me. How lucky I have been to eat nutritious food and drink clean water every day. How lucky I have been to look out of my window and see the sky and the trees and to tend a little garden. How lucky I have been to learn how to be quiet inside and not to make myself feel good by making others feel bad. How lucky I have been to read and write, to sing and dance, to laugh and play.

Chapter Five

On How My Mum and Dad Got Together
Part One

My father was born in the small village of Kobern-Gondorf on the Mosel River near the Deutches Eck, where the Mosel and the Rhine meet. The nearest large town is Koblenz. It is a lovely part of Germany, wine country, where the grape vines grow in the porous slate soil on the steep slopes of the river. There has been a Jewish community in Kobern for centuries. I was told that the shul was on one side of the river and the Jews who lived on the other side were given special religious dispensation to cross the river by ferry on Shabbos, as long as they stood still for the entire journey. I hope this story is true.

Dad's father, Gustav Windmüller was born in the small town of Rodenberg, near Hannover, on October 29th 1885 and he married Paula Grunewald on March 8th 1920. Now my Dad's birthday is January 15th 1920, so Dad was born before they were married. Tragically, Paula died at home, November 6th 1920, from blood poisoning after an abortion, not even ten months after my Dad was born. I discovered this only recently and I wonder if they knew she was pregnant again when they married, or if Paula even told Gustav?

She was buried in the little local Jewish cemetery in Rodenberg, a ten minute walk from their house in Langestrasse, along a winding, leafy lane. It is surrounded by trees and bushes. Gustav's mother, Yetta/Jettchen/Henriette is also buried there. Gustav married again in 1921 to Else/Elise Fischbach from Meinerzhagen and Dad's half brother Oskar was born on March 27th 1922 in Rodenberg.

Grandpa Gustav did not tell Dad about his real mother, Paula, until he was thirteen. Maybe the intention to keep Paula secret from Dad was part of an attempt to hide a scandal. I will never know.

Paula was born on September 18th, 1891, in Kobern, where she lived with her parents, Samuel Grunewald and Susanne Mayer. She was known as Blümchen or Little Flower.

Samuel was a merchant. He was born in Waldgirmes, in 1858 and was the head of the small Kobern Jewish community.

Susanne was born in 1854. They were married in 1890 and lived on 10 Muhlengraben. Susanne was Samuel's second wife. When Samuel died in 1933, their son Julius, who was a cattle dealer, supported Susanne and his younger sister, Selma. In 1935, Selma was denounced by a neighbour because she was heard being critical of the Nazis, but the case was dropped by a Cologne special court.

In 1936, Julius was accused by the Nazis of swearing a false oath on an insurance contract with a farmer's widow. It was a favourite Nazi harassing tactic. He was sent to prison for six months. On his release in 1937, he couldn't take the abuse anymore and decided to leave the country with his wife and daughter. All his property was forfeited to the state and Susanne and Selma lost their home and source of income.

In August 1938, Susanne was accused by the local police of running an illegal boarding house for Jews. By now they were living on welfare, but in January 1939 that was stopped and they relied on handouts. In August 1939, Susanne was accused by local police of associating with men of German blood and in October 1939 they were both moved to Dusseldorf. Selma was taken into a "Jewish House" where Jews were forced to live in a confined and unsanitary space. She was made to do compulsory hard labour. Susanne was put up in a charity home run by the local Jewish community.

In June 1940, Selma was sent to Dusseldorf prison. Then later in the year she was moved to Ravensbruck, a concentration camp for women. In November 1940, she was sent to Leipzig prison and within a few weeks back to Ravensbruck. In May 1942, Susanne was informed that Selma had died on the 15th. She was murdered by gassing as part of the "Sondederbehandlung 14f13" programme in the killing facility at Bernburg Hospital on the Saale.

My Great Grandma Susanne was taken by train to the ghetto/camp at Theresienstadt in Czechoslovakia on 21st July 1942. She died there aged eighty eight on 28th October 1942.

In the 1930s, Grandpa Gustav had a butcher's shop in Rodenberg. His in-laws, the Fischbachs, were also in the cattle business like Julius. As many Jews did, Gustav fought for Germany in the First World War. I have a photograph of him in uniform looking very Prussian. They were fairly wealthy. Dad told me that they had monogrammed silver cutlery and that he had his own horse. Gustav was very old fashioned and would not use motor vehicles at all so they travelled by horse and trap. Their property was a large three story building, six windows wide and had living quarters for staff as well as the family. The shop was on the ground floor with stables behind, and every winter they would build an ice house that would last well into the summer months.

They believed, as many German Jews did, that they were truly German and integrated into society. After all there had been Windmüllers in Germany since 1680. I have a copy of the "Family Book", "The Windmüller Family Chronicle" which lists, to the present day, all the descendents, and their wives and children, of Levi Windmüller who lived in Warendorf, North-Rhine, Westphalia all that time ago.

The Windmüllers were a large family, and though some escaped Germany, over one hundred and twenty of the extended family died in the Holocaust.

Dad was not allowed to go to school in the 1930s, and had his barmitzvah in secret, with guards outside, in January 1933, a few days before Hitler was declared chancellor. It was on his barmitzvah that he was told that Else was not his biological mother and about Paula's death.

Gustav refused to believe that they would be in danger but after Kristallnacht, also known as Pogromnacht, in November 1938, when Jews were attacked and Jewish property burned all over Germany, he was detained by the local police and it was obvious that events were only going to get worse. In Kobern the shul was set alight and when the fire brigade tried to put it out they were attacked by the local Nazis.

So Gustav sold his business and property in Rodenberg. They took advantage of his desperation and paid him a ridiculously small amount. The money was paid into his bank but like many Jews his account was "blocked" which meant he was only able to draw small monthly amounts. Once the war began the whole amount was confiscated by the Nazis as part of the "Arisierung" or "Aryanisation" of Germany. In the late 1930s, there were only three Jewish families living in Rodenberg and they were being constantly harassed by the police. One tactic was to inflame local public opinion on false accusations of "Madchenschadung" ("girl abuse").

In July 2014, the artist Gunter Demnig placed three "Stolpersteine" or stumbling stones, in commemoration of Gustav, Else and Oskar in front of their house at 23 Lange Strasse in Rodenberg. There are now over 56,000 stolpersteine across Europe.

On November 30th 1938, Gustav and Else moved to the "Israelitische Gartenbauschule Ahlem", the Jewish Horticultural School, near Hannover, where Oskar had been a horticultural student since January 1936. Dad told me that Oskar was always interested in horticulture and that his ambition was to go to Holland to study the ways they cultivated bulbs.

I have photographs of Gustav and Oskar in the kitchens at Ahlem pictured with large metal vats. I also have a photograph of Dad, Oskar, and a young man, possibly another student, Helmut Bloch. Dad had already moved there 19th March 1937 and worked as a Hausgehilfe, a general domestic worker or home help.

Until early 1942, Jews were relatively safe in Ahlem as by then it was mostly being used as a centre for the deportation of Jews abroad, and as it was a private school the banning of Jews from education did not yet apply. Maybe that was why Gustav and Else thought it was a good idea to go there. Also the director of Ahlem, Leo Rosenblatt, was related to Henriette Rosenblatt, Dad's other Grandma. Leo's father, Daniel, and Henriette were brother and sister. They were both born in Beisefoerth in Hessen. This could be another reason Gustav and Elsa moved to Ahlem.

Gustav, Elsa and Oskar were not at Ahlem consistently. In August of 1940 Gustav moved first to Koblenz then to Weisbaden returning to Ahlem after a month. Elsa moved to Pohle near Rodenberg for most of July 1940 and Oskar worked as a gardener in Hannover from March 1940 to September 1941 when he was sent to the "Judenhaus" in Berger Strasse which was the old shul. Hannover was being bombed and property was at a premium so any remaining Jews were evicted from their homes to make way for "proper" Germans and packed into tiny overcrowded spaces. Oskar returned to Ahlem at the end of November 1941 along with other Jews from Hannover.

Around the time of Kristallnacht, Dad, and his cousin, Heinz Hans Grunewald, were on a biking holiday to visit his relatives in Kobern. On the way, Dad and Heinz were both arrested in the town of Herdecke by the Dortmund police and taken to Sachsenhausen-Oranienburg concentration camp near Berlin. At that time, it was mostly for political prisoners like communists and for vagrants and gypsies. More Jews were taken there after Kristallnacht. He said that for a while the man who slept next to him was a Jewish scientist who had been involved in the creation of synthetic rubber known as buna, which was important for the war effort. Heinz lost fingers from frostbite. This was from the interminable roll-calls of the prisoners who were made to stand outside, sometimes for days, while they were checked and re-checked in freezing temperatures. If someone fell and you tried to help them, you would be shot. Heinz killed himself in 1954 by jumping off a skyscraper in New York. These terrible and traumatic experiences affected people in different ways. My Dad coped by making himself a new life and a new family in England.

As the Nazis became more and more powerful, Jews were sacked from academia and scientific research projects. A whole range of restrictions gradually came into force. They could not vote and were deprived of all civil rights. Jews were not allowed in public parks, on public transport, in cinemas, sports venues or theatres. Jewish businesses were seized and sold off at well below market value. Jewish doctors were not allowed to treat "Aryans" and Jewish lawyers had their licence to practice revoked. They were barred from all professions and expelled from the civil service. Jewish men had to add Israel to their name and Jewish women likewise had to add Sarah. Jews were beaten up and humiliated in the streets, and it became dangerous to go out at all.

Dad did not talk much about his experiences in Sachsenhausen. He told me how you couldn't know, until it counted, who was going to share with others, whether it was food or some scrap of something. He said some of the most religious were the most selfish. He told Mum that in 1939 he was just "kicked out", and was convinced he had some kind of outside help.

I have information from Sachsenhausen that he was registered there as prisoner number 11708 and housed in block 18. He was released from the camp on 9th January 1939, back to Dortmund. Most of the files were destroyed by the SS before the evacuation of the camp. There are still some records in the archives of the Russian Federation which I have not yet accessed. He made his way back to Ahlem, about 250 miles, and on the way was sheltered by people and hidden in their barns. Ahlem has recently sent me several documents from this time period about his application to leave. Included is an inventory of the clothes and belongings that he was taking with him to England which had to be submitted to the local Gestapo. Gustav took a loan of 400 RM to finance the trip. There are also two letters from Gustav about Dad's bicycle which I find very moving.

"Ahlem 30 June 1939
53717
To The Chief Financial Officer of the Foreign Exchange, Hannover.

At the end of April/beginning of May, there was an Approved Removal Item List for my son Hans Israel Windmüller, who since the previous month is an agricultural assistant in Dungannow (sic) Tyrone Northern Ireland. Subsequently I ask for permission to send to my son a bike, F. W. B. Bike Works, Bismark, with a lamp and air pump (value perhaps RM 20.--) which has been in his possession since 1934.

Gustav Israel Windmüller"

"Customs Office I Weidendamm
22 October 1940 35568 Z 2401 B-B

"Due to the instructions of Mr. OFPras. Hannover on 11.9.40 Z 2401 A - 56 Z 203 I inform you that a bicycle destined for export to Northern Ireland by the Jew Gustav Israel Windmüller in Hannover - Limmer - Gartenbauschule Ahlem (kenn - Nr A 0065) for export to Northern Ireland was held in Bremen due to the outbreak of war and has been returned from there in June 1940. On the basis of the authorization granted to the Principal Officer of Hannover by means of the above mentioned arrangement, the bicycle was taken to the Jew on September 27, 1940, for the sake of equity (fairness). The authorization to export the bicycles is from 10.7.1939 B 1/53117 or 53717

To the Chief Financial Officer
(Foreign exchange)"

Even though their own situation was perilous, Gustav and Else wanted to send my Dad the bike that he had owned since 1934. The tone of the reply, which is not sent directly to Gustav but to some official, refers to Gustav as "The Jew". The racism is horribly casual and the reason given for the bike's eventual return as "fairness" is both ironic and appalling, because a few years later they were murdered in Auschwitz.

On May 5th 1939, Dad sailed on the Europa from Bremen and arrived in Southampton the next day. He brought a big black trunk, with his name stencilled on it, that contained the personal effects listed in his application. He was still underweight and unwell, and he lived unhappily in London for a while with no money and little English. He said he was still getting used to sleeping in a bed again, and he would often sleep on the floor. Gradually he learned English from a book.

I surmise that in Ahlem, Gustav and Else told my Dad to go ahead without them and that they would follow and join him later. Like many others they parted with hopes that were never realised. If they had all survived, then I would not be alive, nor would my daughter or grandchildren. I really owe my life to them.

I have seen a film called "The Locket" by Margaret Fischbach Bilinsky, funded by Steven Spielberg. It's about the Fischbach family, those who escaped Nazi Germany and those who did not. Else, my step-Grandma was a Fischbach, and Margaret's Auntie.

One scene in the film shows a postcard sent to Margaret's father, Oskar Fischbach, in the USA, by Gustav and Else from Ahlem. It is dated 14th February 1941.

"My Dears,
We very much hope you have received our airmail letters.
We received some mail yesterday from my brother Max. In it he promises to help out so that our exit paperwork can soon be sent. I beg you dear Oskar, to get in touch with Max, so that everything can be sorted out for us. As we told you our waiting number from the American Consul General has been called and I beg you from the bottom of my heart to speed things up as we would like to move there as quickly as possible.
With heartfelt greetings
Gustav and Else. "

I also discovered a book "A Final Reckoning", by Ruth Gutmann in which she relates being sent to Ahlem in June 1942. She mentions Oskar Windmüller, my Dad's brother, as being one of two remaining students, and that Oskar's parents also lived there. By the time she arrived most of the staff and residents were already gone. It was closed by the end of 1942, early 1943. When the Gestapo headquarters in Hannover was bombed, they took over Ahlem. It later became a concentration camp. It is now a memorial.

I was shocked to read the account by Ruth as I was researching the school at Ahlem, and had not expected to see Oskar and my Grandparents mentioned in a book. Likewise the postcard from Gustav and Else really moves me because they still had some hope in 1941 that they were close to being able to escape, and because of their obvious desperation.

However, they were still in Ahlem in June 1942, and on March 2nd 1943 they were all transported directly to Auschwitz, nearly four years after my Dad escaped to England. Ahlem supplied me with the train orders. Susan, my sister, remembers that my Dad told her he did manage to have some contact with his parents up to 1942.

In London, he was contacted by an organisation called "Hechalutz", or "Pioneer", which was a left wing Zionist organisation set up to teach agriculture to young Jews with the intention of them eventually going to Israel to cultivate the land. Gustav was trying to send Dad's bike to Northern Ireland in June of 1939 only a month after Dad left Germany so he was only in London for a few weeks. So by that time Dad was working on a farm in Dungorman Road, Moy, near Dungannon in Co Tyrone, Northern Ireland. He told me it was just what he needed. Being outside, in touch with nature, working the land, all helped him to heal.

The farmer's name was William Frederick Hazelton. Dad was not paid in wages but with food and board, a similar arrangement to his stay at Ahlem. He told me that one of the questions he was often asked in Ireland was about his religion. When he told them he was a Jew, the next question was, "Are you a Catholic Jew or a Protestant Jew?" The answer had to be the right one.

In 1940, the British Government had a policy of internment for "Enemy Aliens"; Germans. The Jewish refugees in Britain had to appear before a court to determine their status and subsequently many were held in camps. The main camp was in the Isle of Man where most of the inmates were Jews. Italians and Austrians were also interned. The British Government didn't comprehend that Jews were not likely to be Nazi sympathisers and that many of them had been in concentration camps. Dad was in court in 1939. I have his "Male Enemy Alien Exemption from Internment – Refugee" certificate, dated 21st October 1939. His normal occupation is given as a butcher and his present occupation as a trainee in farming. With the support of the Chief Rabbi of Ireland, he managed to be classified as a "Friendly Enemy Alien" and so was not put in a camp. His name is recorded as Hans Israel Windmüller. The Nazi law that Jewish men must add "Israel" to their names was passed August 17th 1938. The added "Israel" must have been on the documents he brought with him from Germany to gain entry into England.

He stayed in Moy for three years, and then went to Manchester and worked in a munitions factory in Trafford Park as a fitter/assembler. He told me he moved to Manchester because he was a fan of Manchester United. By now he could speak English but with an Irish twang. He lived in various lodgings until he joined the Habonim, another left-wing Zionist group, and he lived communally in the "Bayit", Hebrew for house. It was situated at 3 Wilton Polygon, Bury Old Road, where later I went to school.

Many of the people there eventually moved to Israel. This is called "Making Aliyah". Dad was supposed to go to Israel as well, but he met Vivi, Mum's younger sister, at a Habonim dance and, through her, met Mum. He proposed to Mum as he was walking her home one night, and they were married barely six months after they met.

They initially married in a registry office on April 11th, 1945, because Dad had joined the British army and was due to be shipped out soon. He had enlisted February 1945, trained in Maidstone, and transferred to the Palestine Regiment in the April. Soon after, he joined The Jewish Brigade which was formed the year before. It consisted of 50,000 men. He changed his name to Dennis Windham on the advice that it would be better for him to have an English name if he was captured in Europe, but he wasn't naturalised as British until 1947.

In the chaos, destruction and darkness of post-war Europe, the Brigade was involved in feeding and illegally transporting over 20,000 freed inmates of the concentration camps to Palestine, using British army equipment and trucks. Palestine was a British mandate and in the end army officials became so irritated with the Brigade's illegal activities that it was disbanded in the summer of 1946. He then joined the Manchester Regiment and I have postcards he sent to Mum from Europe. One is from Udine, Italy, August 1945, another from Antwerp, October 1945, and one from Bielefeld in Germany in November 1946, as well as others without a date.

He broke his lower femur in May 1945 and spent some time in hospital. I also have a photograph of him taken at Belsen Concentration Camp. It is of two football teams posing after a match. The inscription reads, "Belsen 26th of September 1946, Poale-Zion v Jewish Brigade". Poale-Zion was a Marxist Zionist Group. The Brigade won 3-2. How my Dad got to Belsen, I do not know. That he was there at all is amazing to me. Belsen was discovered and liberated April 15th 1945. Even after the camps were liberated some survivors stayed as they had nowhere else to go and or were just too ill to move.

He sent an audio message to my Mum on a 5" record. Soldiers' messages were recorded at Naafi clubs across Europe, and transferred onto an aluminium disc coated with shellac. They cost one shilling and ninepence, and were sent to the soldier's loved ones in a special envelope. The record label reads "Voices of the Forces Postal Record, Organised by Army Welfare, Naafi & Ensa". It is a touching recording. He is obviously reading from a prepared script, and says how much he loves and misses Mum. He says that he is in Villach, in Austria and I have a photograph of him in Villach dated August 2nd 1945 so I presume that is the date of the recording.

Mum told me that on his first leave in 1945, she travelled down to London by train to see him, and that Grandma said "You've only been married in a registry office, not in shul, so don't sleep with him". Their shul wedding was on December 5th 1945.

He was naturalised as British on 7th November 1947 under the British Nationality and Status of Aliens Act 1914. As Mum had married Dad while he was still a German citizen, she became officially German, and she was naturalised British again on 6th November 1946. She received the "Certificate of Naturalisation granted to a woman who was at birth a British Subject and is married to a subject of a State at War with His Majesty". She also had to swear an oath of allegiance to the King. Interestingly on the certificate "name of husband" is given as, "Dennis Windham, otherwise Hans Jakob Israel Windmüller". I presume both Jacob and Israel were added by the Nazis. I have a document from Winningen, which is the municipality of my Dad's birthplace, Kobern, as follows:

"Winningen 10th September 1938
The father of the child mentioned here, acting as his legal representative, has given notice that the said child will henceforth be known as "Israel"
Winningen 13th July 1945
In accordance with the law No 1, Article 1, Paragraph G of the Military Government, the margin note provided above concerning the adoption of the forename "Israel" has been declared invalid"

I can only guess how Gustav, my grandfather, felt when he had to give his permission for this. Invalidating it is a hollow victory.

One cold, damp and dark winter's evening, when I was nine, I was walking home from a Bible lesson, when I hear a dog whimpering. It was a little dog shivering in a shop doorway. I felt sorry for it and picked it up. It snuggled into my coat for warmth. I read the address on its collar and walked about ten minutes to a dark house. I knocked on the door and a man answered. He recognised the dog, muttered how he was always getting out, and closed the door. I went home and told Mum why I was late. She said,

"So you do have a heart after all".

This incident has stayed with me all these years. At the time, I had never considered whether I did have a heart or what it meant, but it made me realise there was such a thing and I had one. I wasn't hurt, more puzzled. In all probability, I had never acted compassionately before. I am sure I was a selfish and manipulative boy, but this small yet pivotal moment awoke me to the possibility of acting altruistically. It also asks the question of why I do what I do. Who is it I am trying to impress in my life? Being a psychotherapist was a perfect way to try to prove to my Mum that in caring for others "I really do have a heart after all"

I have identified with and maintained that position for years. I was acting from it, perceiving the world through it, and believing without questioning that it was me.

How attractive it is to imagine that even though my daughter and my grandchildren have not had the same life experiences as me that they should know what I know. People today still want the same, to have enough to eat, to be happy, to be fulfilled, and to have some control. The toys that we play with have evolved but we have not. Is there more violence in the world? Is this some special time in history? I think not. Sheer weight of numbers contributes to the quantity of pain that we inflict on each other as well as the speed of reporting. Throughout history, the majority of people have been involved in one war or another and lived and died in squalor. I have been fortunate not to have fought in a war but that is a blip, an anomaly. The usual situation is conflicts of power around ideology, religion and economics and that never really went away.

Chapter Six

On How My Mum and Dad Got Together
Part Two

Mum was born November 24th 1923 in 13 St. James' Road, Broughton, Salford, the same place we lived just after I was born. Twenty five years later somehow she had gone back there after living with her parents in Elizabeth Street. Her first name was Syrilla, which she never liked. She preferred to be called Rosie by the family. Dad's special names for her were "Heppy" or "Mutti".

Mum was always a worrier and very shy. She and her younger sister, Vivi, were close as children and they didn't have many other friends. Mum always wanted to be a teacher and from quite a young age she would set up a classroom in her bedroom with make-believe desks, teach a class and give them homework, which she would mark. I only know of one instance of a mishap which was when she was nine or ten. It was a hot summer and she had a very itchy insect bite on her bottom, so she filled the sink with cold water and sat in it to cool off. The sink came away from the wall and flooded the room.

She went to the Jewish school on Waterloo Road, from infant to junior, then to Manchester Central High School for Girls. She was a Hebrew scholar, which was very unusual for a girl in those days, and she attended the local Talmud Torah on Bent Street, as well as being academic at school. At fourteen she was awarded the Intermediate Certificate for Hebrew and Religious Knowledge from Jews College in London and The Proficiency in Hebrew Speaking Certificate from the Talmud Torah Trust. Aged sixteen she was the first girl to win a major prize at the Talmud Torah, and travelled down by train to London with the headmaster, Dr Judah Slotki, to be presented to the Chief Rabbi. They were verbally abused on the journey. Slotki was an easy target because of his clothes and beard. Her prize was "The Jewish Religion", a book by Michael Friedlander. In the local Jewish press, when it was reported, she was not even named, just "a girl won the prize."

Mum began secondary school at Central High on Whitworth Street in 1934. She was expected to go to Manchester High but didn't take the entrance exam. She attended an assessment first with a large group of other girls and one of the first questions was on geography. A map of a country was shown with no markings and the girls were asked to name the country and anything they knew about it. As the country was Israel, Mum instantly recognised it, and could have given a long lecture on the subject, but she was so nervous she could not speak. I imagine she had something like a panic attack. This put her off for the rest of the day.

She told me that she was very happy at Central High. She passed her School Certificate in July 1940 in six subjects and her Higher in July 1942. Manchester High was a much posher school and has many well known alumni. Auntie Vivi went there two years later and did not enjoy it. She was bullied for being one of the poorer kids and for what she wore.

Mum was accepted at Leeds Carnegie Teachers Training College in 1942, but she never actually studied there. That year the college was requisitioned as a military hospital and the students and staff were evacuated to Scarborough on the north Yorkshire coast. Some of the female students were billeted in the Red Lee Hotel on Prince of Wales Terrace. The hotel is still there. She had a very different life there than she had known in Manchester. She was eighteen and free.

There were several thousand children evacuees from Hull and Hartlepool and a few from the South East. More importantly there were also a few thousand servicemen. The town became restricted to visitors and there were military checkpoints on all roads in and out. There was a black-out at night and some bombs were dropped causing casualties.

Given this potent mixture, and like elsewhere at this time, the young people had a good time while they could. Mum was no exception, and I know of at least one boyfriend she had, Jacques, a French airman. Even more amazing, he was not Jewish. I have several pictures of her posing happily with fellow students in their striped blazers, but none with men. Maybe she didn't want it recorded. She told me that she studied Walt Whitman and that her favourite book she wrote about for a project was his "Leaves of Grass".

Mum was a very private person. Although she was fantastic with children, she was not socially skilled with adults. She was shy until provoked. Once she had her own family, she preferred to be at home with them. Her favourite film star was Tyrone Power and she loved the music of the Great American Songbook. As a teenager, she was a real film fan and would go to the pictures two or three times a week. She had scrapbooks full of photos of her favourite stars. When she returned home from college she was horrified to discover that Grandma had thrown them all out.

We didn't have a record player in Manchester but we had the radio and our house was always filled with music, mostly her singing. She had a lovely voice, and through her I learned to love the music and lyrics of Cole Porter, George Gershwin, Irving Berlin and all those great songwriters. I learned how songs were constructed and how lyrics must bounce on the line. They became part of my blood well before I was seduced by the blues and rock 'n' roll.

One of my most treasured possessions is a small aluminium record she made in a booth on the sea front at Blackpool, of the lullaby "Go To Sleep My Baby". When we were older and living in Southport, she bought a tape recorder and recorded an hour of her singing that she played for us when we went to bed. She would start singing to us live, and then she would switch the tape on as we were falling asleep. I wish I had that tape now. I would put it on a CD or a stick and use it to help my grandson go to sleep.

After a while my carefree days with my Grandparents came to an end and Mum started me at school. She had passed her probation in 1946. Naturally she had become an infant teacher and in those days class size was often fifty plus. She took me to some of the schools where she worked, Webster Street in Moss Side, Alfred Street in Harpurhey in February 1952, and Crumpsall Infants School. I have pictures of her posing with her classes in that classic school photo way. She looks so fresh and young and eager.

Those school days were a great mystery to me, mainly because I came into contact with working class kids who were not Jewish. Hightown was a working class Jewish area and we mixed mostly with other Jews. These kids were Christians and it was like visiting another world, but always being the visitor.

The schools were poor but I didn't know that. I remember the little cracked wash basins with only cold water, child size toilets in rows, and the shiny non-absorbent toilet paper. The brands were Izal and Bronco. Izal was medicated and smelled funny. I never did figure out how you were supposed to wipe yourself with it. Even newspaper was preferable.

In the winter, even though the schools were heated by a boiler, my nose would get cold. We were warmed up by doing exercises, mostly star jumps. You only got really warm if you sat next to a radiator. Going to the toilet became a race to get back to the classroom because the toilets were not deemed worth heating. At home was the warmth and certainties of Jewishness, where Mum was the centre of my world.

I never really appreciated being young. I did enjoy lots of sports like rugby, swimming and squash but it was so usual I somehow missed the suchness of it. For the most part my body worked well. If I got an ache or a cold it was something that would just pass. Now every little pain has import for me in what it might mean. When I was a teenager a rock-hard erection that wouldn't go away could be an annoying embarrassment. Nowadays, keeping anything up for any length of time is an achievement.

Being old and getting older is a tremendous challenge. I watch and feel my body deteriorate. I fear getting into the clutches of the doctors. I am not ready to leave but I know that it is not my choice. So I give it my best shot to enjoy every moment knowing that it may be my last, to love the ones I love and who love me, to keep my little flame burning for as long as I can.

Chapter Seven

Southport

We moved to Southport in October 1954. Dad bought the local kosher butcher shop on the corner of 14 Hill Street and Anchor Street from Joe Max. The shop front was on Hill Street but the front door to the house was on Anchor Street. The shop next door changed hands several times over the years, but the one I remember best was when it was a carpet shop owned by Mr. and Mrs. Black.

Our house was a long narrow building with a yard at the back and a shed. If you went through the front door, to the right was a door directly into the back of the shop, immediately straight ahead were stairs up to the three bedrooms and to the left was the living room with a suite, a fireplace and a TV, then a largish kitchen where Mum cooked and we ate. There was a back door into the yard. We hung our coats on the back door. Upstairs, to the right, was my parents' room, overlooking Hill Street with a bay window and a little veranda. To the left were two bedrooms, and then at the end of the corridor was the bathroom and toilet. Stephen and I slept in the first bedroom and when Paul was born in February 1956, I moved to the second bedroom and Paul went in with Stephen.

Dad loved being a kosher butcher and working for himself. It meant Mum could give up teaching and be the full-time Mum she wanted to be, but more than that it established a living link to his lost family in Germany. The shop itself was very old fashioned. There were two worn butcher blocks, and a work table. The only refrigeration was a small walk-in fridge at the back. There were steel rails on the walls with various size hooks, and worn cleavers and saws there hung menacingly.

Dad was extremely strict about both hygiene and kashrus (Jewish dietary laws). Unlike most other butchers of the day, he would not have sawdust on the floor. He had two butchers who worked for him George Whipp and Norman Forshaw. They stayed with him for years. There was another man who worked part time, called Granville, who was also a coalman. We sometimes visited him in Bolton where he lived.

How proud we all were when the sign writer put his name on the shop window, "D Windham Kosher Butcher and Poulterer" in big red script.

Meat was still on ration and customers had to be signed up to a particular shop. Some of the customers were used to getting a bit under the counter for cash, but Dad would have none of it. Some, though not all, were businessmen, entrepreneurs who had risen from their poor immigrant backgrounds. It was their children who were being educated and who would become professionals; doctors, dentists, lawyers and solicitors or something in the arts.

The daily train from Southport to Manchester was the Jewish businessman's commute. The trains were old-fashioned with corridors and slam-doors, and there were card schools that lasted the hour long journey to Victoria station. They gossiped, told jokes, and boasted about their holidays to Europe and how well their children were doing. This was well before the advent of package holidays.

Many of their parents and grandparents had fled the pogroms in Eastern Europe, and the nouveau-riche element hid their guilt over owning flash cars and living in big houses in the best areas of town like Birkdale and Hillside. Some lived near the golf course that did not allow Jews in as members. The big houses had been built by rich merchants who had factories in Manchester and Liverpool. In the 50s, alcohol was the drug of choice and cocktail parties were the rage.

Many aspired to the American celebrity lifestyles that Frank Sinatra, Dean Martin and Perry Como sang about, and all that represented in terms of money, fashion, sex, and living the good life. However, Dad being the butcher did not fit well into this image. This did not affect me that much when I became a teenager, but there were certain social doors that were closed to Mum and Dad. There are different clubs in every walk of life and different admission rules. There are clubs for those who are wealthy and those not so wealthy, clubs for those who are frum and those not so frum.

Of course, being six, I knew none of this or its wider ramifications. My world was made of my new house, my new school and the consequences of that. Having a bathroom with a bath and a toilet was pretty luxurious. My parents bought a new floral pattern suite for the living room with a high-backed winged armchair. Gradually, we got a new cooker with an eye-level grill and a washing machine and a new telly. We became modern. We soon settled into a routine and I felt more at home.

Food was a big part of this. Mondays meant braised steak, potatoes, peas and carrots. There was never any gravy though. We would ask Mum where the gravy had gone, and she would always say that it had gone into the meat. Mum's style of cooking meat could be describes as "gedempte" which generally means a slow pot roast but more often means overcooked. It was a long standing source of amusement. Tuesday was grilled chops with the same veggies; Wednesdays roast chicken; Thursdays fish; Fridays chicken soup and chicken; Saturday lunch chicken; Sundays picklemeat, vorsht, eggs, and viennas. Sometimes we had egg on toast for a treat

Dad would often fry steak and onions seasoned with paprika. He liked a dish he made for himself which was sliced tomatoes and sliced cucumber marinaded for several days in vinegar and sugar. Lunch was a free-for-all, consisting of salad, cheeses, tinned salmon and bread. When I say salad I mean tomatoes, cucumber and lettuce. Peppers and avocados, for example, hadn't arrived in England yet. Fruit was what was in season.

We had a weekly delivery of what we called "Pop", sugary carbonated drinks. We would have a wooden crate a week. The delivery man always announced himself at the back door, "Pools Beverages!" he would shout. At first it was in stone bottles but then glass. We had orange, dandelion and burdock and cream soda. We also drank the cordial Vimto, hot and cold. At some point, we changed to Aerowater Minerals who had a factory and a car park on Warwick Road near Man United's ground, and as a customer, Dad got a ticket to park there on match days. Warwick Road was in one of the songs the United fans sang to the tune of "Blaydon Races".

"Oh me lads,
You should have seen em comin,
Fastest team in the league,
Just to see us runnin,
All the lads and lasses
With smiles upon their faces,
Walking down the Warwick Road,
To see Matt Busby's aces."

Dad also liked drinking little bottles of Schweppes bitter lemon and we kept them in the fridge. As a treat Mum would get a box of cakes from Matti and Tissot on Lord Street and we would eat them with a bottle of cold bitter lemon. Vanilla slices were the best. I also liked Tizer (the appetiser). When my Grandparents returned from America, Grandpa began drinking 7Up. I spent hours trying to figure how the name should be pronounced.

Supermarkets were in the future and shopping meant going to several different shops. I remember the grocer on Hill Street and actually paying with farthings. Moors Market, on Houghton Street, which later became an early "stack em high and sell it cheap" Tesco's, was one of the earliest trials at being a supermarket.

Apparently, I was a naughty boy, and in those days that meant being smacked, which seemed to happen a lot to me. The time I remember best was when I covered the back yard in ant powder. We had an infestation of ants and they were all over the yard and coming into the kitchen so Mum bough a large pack of ant powder to kill them. I saw the ant powder and decided I would do it, and spread the entire contents of the pack over the yard and the inside of the shed. I got told off and smacked for this. Mum kept the letter that I wrote to her about it in May 1956, in her photo album, I was eight. She called it a "conscience letter".

"Dear Mummy
I am all-ways trying to be help-full and then evrey thing gose rong and you shout at me and smack me, Like the time when I sprinkled the yard with ant-powder
Love from Geoffrey xxx

But it wasn't a conscience letter at all; it was my sense of indignation that my best efforts were only acknowledged with me being told off.

School was difficult at first. My new school was a Church of England school called Holy Trinity named after the large church next to which it stood. The school blazer was the first confusion for me or more accurately the badge on the blazer. It was a symbol of the Holy Trinity, something of which I had no knowledge, a triangle inverted in another triangle a six pointed hexagram. I was confused because it was the same symbol on the badge of the King David School. It was the Magen Dovid, the Star of David, the flag of Israel, to me it was Jewish.

Every morning began with an assembly and prayers. There were about six or seven Jewish kids in the whole school and we stood outside until the prayers were over and then we were led in and stared at in silence as we found our places with our classmates. We waited in a small vestibule at the top of several stone steps in front of two very large, very heavy, wooden swing doors that opened into the main hall. The door edges were shiny and worn from years of small hands.

On the first day, I heard this strange singing, followed by spoken words that I did not understand, and then the doors were opened and in we went under the scrutiny of hundreds of eyes. So on the second day, I peeked through the gap in the doors and they were singing like we sang in shul, but nothing like we sang in shul. It was all high and prim and cold. I thought it was the sound of being English and I knew it wasn't me. Then they all put their hands together, and I heard,

"Our father, witch art in Heaven"

and,

"Thy will be done on Earth as it is in Heaven"

What did that mean? Did they think there were witches in heaven? Who was this father? And what was it that will be done? I had not heard of "will" being a noun.

The playground was old fashioned, paved and surrounded by a high brick wall. On the first day, Jan Faber, who was the older brother of Charlie, later to be my friend, sought me out and kicked me to remind me who was boss. I didn't kick back, he was much, much bigger than me, and he had an aura of toughness that spoke more than the kick. It was just one to suffer. Anyway, some of the boys were kicking a small ball around and they let me join in.

The classrooms were on the first floor and there seemed to be so many windy stairs and corridors. When the bell rang and it was time to go in I just followed others who were in my class. The two boys that were most friendly to me were Jewish kids, Julian Desser and Laurence Berg. They showed me around, and we were friends right through school and beyond. Julian's father, Maurice sold baskets wholesale.

The rooms were joined, so from one end it was up the stairs and on the left the Headmaster's, Mr Tebble's, office, then through a door to 1a, then through the classroom to 2a, then to 3a, then to 4a. Each classroom was partitioned from the next by a wall whose bottom half was wooden and whose top half was frosted glass. They were not noise proof. The desks were individual wooden antiques with an inkwell top right. Inside the lid were carvings from previous occupants. Being a "W", I was alphabetically discriminated against and my seat was at the back of the room.

We had to be quiet in class and when the teacher, Mrs Roberts, made an especially important announcement, we were told to sit up straight with arms crossed. This was new to me, fresh from the informal atmosphere of a Jewish class of kids. I soon found that I was quite clever and that my previous education had been superior, so I was a bit ahead. My first year went mostly without incident.

My one regret was that my parents forbade me to play football on Shabbos. Saturday was when the school teams played against other schools, so I couldn't play with the best players because they knew I wouldn't be able to play in the team. I was left to play with the also–rans and I soon lost interest.

The teacher in the second year was Mrs Moreland. She was prissy with a bee-hive hairdo that she was always checking in a little hand mirror. She didn't like me and I didn't like her. Mum went several times to school to complain about her treatment of me. Mum felt justified because as a teacher she knew what was talking about and was convinced Mrs Moreland was a yidden feint.

In 2a, we were supposed to be able to write in ink, but not with fountain pens. The inkwell was filled by the ink monitor and we were given what we called "dippy in pens". I am left handed and the first problem was that the inkwell was on the top right of the desk. I found it almost impossible not to drip ink, after dipping in, as I had to lean across the desk from the left and then bring it all the way back. The second problem was that as a left hander rather than pulling the pen from left to right as I wrote, I had to push it from left to right, often causing the points of the pen nib to open, and more mess. They were cheap pens. I loved it when we were allowed biros. I still don't like writing by hand.

Every Wednesday afternoon was art. On one Wednesday, Mrs Moreland brought in big sheets of white paper and we had poster paints. She handed them out and asked us to paint an outdoor scene. Mum had always encouraged me to draw and paint although I had no talent as an artist, I quite enjoyed it. I decided I would paint a winter night scene in the snow. In the centre I painted a large tree with no leaves and snow on its bare branches. There was snow on the ground and a yellow crescent moon in the sky. I thought about the colour of the tree and decided that a very dark blue would show it was night. I was pleased with it. The end of the lesson arrived and we all handed in our work.

The next Wednesday it was art again and the teacher brought in all our paintings. I could see mine was on the top. She held it up and said,

"Now class I want you to look at this carefully. This is how not to paint. Have you ever seen a blue tree?"

Shamelessly, she shamed me. This incident really put me off painting or drawing. Interestingly, in the 1960s I had friends who went to art school, and I married an artist. I wouldn't say it stopped me being an artist but she certainly helped me to realise my lack of artistic ability, albeit in a very cruel way. I have found other outlets for my creativity in writing and music. In songs and poems that I have written, I have deliberately used the image of blue trees.

I don't remember much of 3a or of the teacher Mr Wright. What really sticks with me is his liberal use of the cane. He hit me on several occasions, I don't even remember why. There was a ritual to all this. The cane and the punishment book were kept in the headmaster's study. I had to go and collect the cane myself. This meant walking through 2a and 1a. Then I had to knock on the headmaster's door.

"Come in", he shouted, in a sing-song way, his voice rising at the end.

"What do you want?"

"I've come to get the cane sir".

The cane, a long whippy wooden stick, was presented to me and I had to carry it back through the other classrooms, and then give it to Mr Wright. I had to hold out my hand and not move it down to minimise the blow. He would hit me three times. Then he handed me the cane and with tears in my eyes I had to walk back through the classrooms, knock on the door, give Mr Tebble the cane back and wait while he filled in the punishment book. Then I had to return. Did it do me any harm? I really don't know. It hurt like hell at the time. I didn't like him at all. In my report for the summer term of 1958, Mr Wright wrote,

"The excellent results attained are marred by the fact that Geoffrey's behaviour is not at all pleasing. We hope you will persuade him to improve in this respect."

Miss Mekin, who taught 3b, was the worst. She had a really mean streak in her. Her preferred punishment was to slap you at the very top of the back of your leg almost on your bottom. To achieve this she would hike up a boy's short trousers or lift a girl's skirt. I only had her a few times when she would stand in, or for geography.

I was more than glad to get into 4a and Mr Johns, who was a proper teacher. He commanded us with kindness, respect and clear boundaries, and I really wanted to do my best for him.

From 2a onwards, I would walk to school and back with Stephen. Like many brothers we fought and I would be mean to him. He remembers me kicking the back of his legs as we walked.

Tuesday afternoon was sport and our sports' ground, The Rookery, was a good twenty minute walk along Manchester Road on Roe Lane, just beyond the railway bridge to Preston. The line was closed down years ago. What seemed like hundreds of us would walk there in a long crocodile, whatever the weather. It was a large field with the usual athletic amenities and a cricket pitch. Whenever I played cricket I just wanted to hit everything. In those days there was little coaching and only the kids who showed natural talent got any attention.

My youngest brother, Paul, was born in February 1956. He was kicking a ball as soon as he could walk and should have had a career as a footballer. He had the same issues of not playing on Saturdays at Holy Trinity but because he was so good they were more than willing to let him play midweek. Southport Boys wanted him to play for them but my parents said no. So when he went to KGV Grammar, and they didn't play football, he missed some important years in his development.

He was a very fast right winger and even though he was the fastest runner in his year and would beat everyone in the inter-house races he was never picked for the school. By then Stephen and I who had been better at rugby, and so accepted, had left KGV. Stephen was a fast runner and a tough rugby player. At fifteen,

Paul played for Southport Amateurs in the Lancashire League which was a high standard. By then my parents had apparently relented.

In his second full season, and aged sixteen, he was playing with and against adults, and he was voted player of the year. He found out later that Manchester City had sent scouts to watch him, which was a big deal in those days, but then he injured his knee and was out for eighteen months. He was given very poor medical advice which made his injury worse. He played again, but sadly he was never the same. My little sister Susan was also a fine footballer but at that time there were no opportunities for women's football. She compensated by going into coaching.

Parallel to my English education was my Jewish education. The shul in Southport was on Arnside Road. It was a lovely old shul full of Italian alabaster and amazing stained glass windows of biblical scenes. At the far end was the Aron Hakodesh where several hand-written scrolls of the Five Books of Moses were kept behind a highly embroidered heavy curtain. To the right was a large carved chair where the Rabbi, Dr Silverstone, sat. He was a big fan of "Gematria" and would often include it in his sermons, which tended to be on the intellectual side. Gematria is an ancient numerical system which codifies letters, words and phrases as numbers and tries to find connections between other letters, words and phrases by dint of their numerical value being the same.

Up above was the choir balcony and further up a stained glass triptych. One of the images was a depiction of the Pillar of Fire by Day and the Pillar of Fire by night that led the Israelites through the desert after the escape from Egypt.

There were two floors and the ladies sat upstairs in the balcony. On both sides were more stained glass windows. In the centre of the ground floor was a large alabaster and wood raised bimah where most of the religious action took place. At the front of the bimah and facing the Aron Hakodesh were seats for the shul executive. They were all men, of course, and they all wore shiny top hats. I always thought that top hats and prayer shawls looked ridiculous. In the 1920s, the Jewish population of Southport was about five hundred, but by the 1950s it has risen to three thousand.

We began to go to shul every Shabbos and soon the service became so familiar to me that I knew it off by heart. My Dad had his own marked seat where he kept his tallis (prayer shawl) and siddurs (prayer books). On most Saturdays the congregation numbered in the low hundreds but on yontavim, the shul would be packed and temporary seating would be put in.

The young ones had to either stand or dodge from seat to seat. Payment for a seat was included in shul membership which also included a payment towards burial costs. The shul secretary was Ivor Freeman; we called him "Freddy". He ran the shul and the services, but trying to organise other Jews as a paid official is not easy. I remember him prowling the bimah during services, glaring at any kids who made a noise or men who talked too loudly, In later years Sam Rosenberg became the shammas and he had a notice made that he would hold up when the noise got too loud, "Decorum Gentlemen Please."

At the back of the shul was the Amelan hall built by a wealthy Southport benefactor Zebulun Louis Amelan. Next to it was the cheder (Hebrew school). The hall was finished in 1954 just as we arrived. At one end was a stage and at the cheder end were the kitchens. I went to cheder Tuesdays and Thursdays straight from school and on Sunday mornings. Thus began my double life in Southport, the religious and the secular. After school, when we arrived at cheder on weekdays, the first thing we did was to go into the kitchen and sit round a large table and eat huge jam butties. This was where I first met Jacqui, my wife's eldest sister, along with Mrs. Cohen, she was one of the volunteer buttie makers. They were made by slicing a huge hunk of white bread and, using the same knife, scooping strawberry jam out of a large stone pot and with the same bread knife, spreading it on the slice of bread.

There were several classes. David Isenberg, Ivor Freeman and Maureen Cohen were some of the teachers. Mrs. Buchalter taught the beginners in the Bes Hamidrash of the shool around a large round, shiny wooden table. We used a book called "Reshis Das" which I think means something like First Knowledge. We learned our alphabet or aleph bet from it.

The headmaster was Reverend Moishe Glazier who was to become a big influence on my life. He was a short stocky man with a little white beard and beady eyes. He loved his religion and he loved teaching children about it. Unfortunately, he and his wife, Kitty, were unable to have children of their own. They adopted a refugee, named Max, who married and moved to Leeds.

Eventually, I was in the top class with Rev Glazier as my teacher. I remember Victor Fagin, Michael Neerkin and Colin Davis as the naughty ones. They were put into a special class of their own because they were so disruptive; they were called "The Untouchables".

Glazier was very old fashioned, although later he mellowed a lot in the way he taught. Most of the lessons consisted of reading the Bible in Hebrew and translating it into English. A mistake could mean a rap on the knuckles with a little stick that he kept for that purpose or a tug and twist of the hair at the top of your neck that really hurt. He kept the stick in his desk and every week we would break into the desk and throw the stick out of the window. Every week he would bring a replacement.

After a couple of years the shul executive decided that Glazier was too old fashioned and that the cheder needed modernising. They sacked him from being headmaster and brought a new man in, Mr. Greenstein. Glazier had become a friend of the family. He was also the town shochet which meant he killed sheep and bullocks at the Southport abattoir, which was on the corner of Poplar Street and Hart Street in Meols Cop.

He was a popular figure with the workers at the abattoir and they all called him "Levi", which although these days might sound racist was strangely more a term of endearment. He was incredibly proud of how keen his knives were and would spend hours sharpening them. There was a large knife for cattle, a medium knife for sheep and lamb, and small one for poultry.

I know there are those who would ban kosher killing in favour of so called humane. There is no humane way to kill and abattoirs are terrible places. I have seen stunning in action and, if I had to choose, kosher would be my preference.

Poultry was killed at Seddon's yard. They were wholesale poulterers, not Jewish, but they had a licence from the shul to sell retail to those who wanted to go to their premises. It was a long shed down a very narrow alley at the back of their house in Blowick. I remember the smell of dead hens being singed on a single gas flame that came from a metal tap on the wall. This was to burn off any remaining feathers and to help remove penkes (stubble).

The men on the shul executive always wanted us to have a competitor for fear we would take advantage of the community. To this end we were forced to compete with Seddon's, our wholesaler. This attitude continued for years and rather than being supportive, they undermined us. They didn't get that next to a shul and a cheder, a kosher butcher is the glue that holds a Jewish community together.

When Rev Glazier was sacked I felt a sense of loyalty towards him and antipathy to the new man. In our living room at Hill Street we had venetian blinds, and one day I was looking through them and saw Mr Greenstein crossing Anchor Street. In an act of solidarity with Rev. Glazier, I stuck my tongue out at Greenstein and then realised he had seen me.

The next day he came round to confront my parents and me. We were in the living room. Mum and Dad flanked me and he stood directly in front of us with his accusations of rudeness and disrespect. He was so angry he stumbled over his words and his face was red. When he had finished Mum turned to me and asked me if I had done it. I lied and denied everything. She said,

"If Geoffrey says he didn't do it, then he didn't!"

I thought he was going to explode. He realised he was not going to get the apology he so wanted. He turned and stormed out. We never spoke of it again.

I learned some things from this. First, that my parents would support me no matter what. Second, that my inner world was truly private and third that telling lies is a very bad thing. Now you might think that I learned that I could get away with telling lies, and I did, but I also learned that it is a hollow victory. Of course, I have lied since and chances are I will again. I am not capable of telling the truth, the whole truth and nothing but the truth all the time.

I never felt the same about cheder again, and eventually stopped going and began to have private lessons with Rev Glazier at his home, in Sussex Road, leading up to him teaching me my barmitzvah. After Greenstein, a new head was appointed called Chaim Alpert, who was an Israeli and lived in Southport on Manchester Road with his family. He was an unkempt man with a thin moustache. I remember his son Yigal, a very thin and gangly boy. Alpert re-organised the cheder, now called Bet Hasepeher, and ran it on more academic lines. The big innovation was to institute a competition, "Pupil of the Year" with a proper awards ceremony, but I never won it.

As a by-product of cheder and shul attendance, I began to make friends with other children in the Jewish community and to visit their homes. I soon realised the difference in levels of affluence.

I rarely had Christian friends home from school, but I did occasionally visit some of them. Peter Taylor was a friend, and sometimes I would hang out with him in his bedroom and listen to music on his Dansette type record player. He had an older sister who was already a teenager; she chewed gum and had a beehive hairdo. He told me that he would spy on her undressing in the bathroom but he never let me join in. His Dad owned a souvenir shop at the top of Neville Street near the promenade. Peter had a Little Richard 45 called "He Got What He Wanted (But He Lost What He Had.)" It's a fantastic gospel type song released on Mercury in 1962, so it was around that date he lent it to me and I never gave it back. Stephen still has it in his Little Richard collection.

I also visited two Jewish friends Barry Samuels and Colin Michaels. Barry lived on Waterloo Road in Birkdale near the golf course. Colin lived with his parents and sister Isabelle on Guilford Road in Ainsdale. Barry's house was a large detached property with a big garden and central heating and really modern kitchen. It was the poshest house I had ever been in. Colin's was more on my level, but it was a house with a garden not attached to a shop. I remained friends with Colin longer than Barry although we did eventually lose contact. He became a dentist and moved to the Manchester area. He was also a regular shul goer and we always sat together and talked about things as if we knew what we were talking about. It was Colin that introduced me to Carole, my wife.

In contrast, Stephen and I began to visit my school friend Charlie Faber in Queens Road. There was a cellar under their house where we would listen to his brother Jan's record collection, the same Jan that kicked me. We only did this when he was away or we would have got more than a kick if he had found out. By now he was a working man, a merchant seaman on the lines that went from Liverpool to New York and back. The records were mostly on the Chess label. We listened to Muddy Waters, Howlin' Wolf, Sonny Boy Williamson, Little Walter and more. Then on the Pye International R&B label, the Bo Diddley and Chuck Berry EPs. We knew nothing about these people, but we loved the music, we loved the singing, we loved the strange lyrics, we loved the crazy rhythm.

We started going on holidays, not abroad at first, but actual holidays. Dad would never close the shop so he would arrive just for the weekend. I had already been on holiday to Lockerbie in Scotland at a Jewish summer school. Stephen and I went by train, a long journey from Southport. I was eight and Stephen six. I have memories of sleeping in a long dormitory and eating communally on long tables. Stephen ruined his shoes playing football on a muddy field.

We went for a day outing to Moffat, and bought something Scottish from a souvenir shop to take home and we walked down the high street eating ice cream cones. When we got home I was told off for not looking after Stephen properly and for the state of his shoes. We hadn't washed much. Other family outings were to Blackpool beach, Ken Dodd shows, and to the Tower Circus where we saw Coco the Clown, walked on the front and had fish and chips in newspaper.

In the summer of 1957 we went to Middleton Towers, a holiday camp on sixty acres near Morecambe bay on the Lancashire coast. It had 900 chalets. The main complex was built like an ocean going liner and was called the SS Berengaria for some reason. It held a two thousand seat theatre. I have vague memories of the ship and mostly remember playing football on the grass near our chalet and anticipating Dad's arrival so we could play together. I entered a Mr. Universe competition where we lined up in our swimming trunks and tried to pose like body builders. I came second. Paul was a toddler but as usual spent most of his time kicking a ball around.

In 1958, my parents bought a small caravan and parked it on a caravan site at Little Budworth near Tarporley in the Cheshire countryside, which was quite a journey from Southport, at least an hour and a half, well before motorways. From Southport we would drive to Widnes then take the transporter across the Mersey to Runcorn, then on to the caravan.

The transporter was a sort of bridge with a moving platform suspended underneath it. The platform was twenty four feet wide and thirty six feet long. It could hold thirty six vehicles and foot passengers. The journey took about four minutes. We always found it an exciting part of a boring journey. It was closed in 1961 and replaced with a new bridge.

Eventually, they bought a larger caravan and parked it at a place called Riverside, in Banks, just outside Southport, where we would stay at the weekend. Dad would be there part-time, either going to a football match or working Sunday morning in the shop. Sometimes my Grandparents would visit for the day. We played board-games or lounged around in deck chairs when it wasn't raining.

In 1960, we went to Butlins at Pwhelli in North Wales. There were eager redcoats and all the silly games they encouraged the campers to do, like knobbly knees competitions, and an indoor raised swimming pool with glass decorated sides so you could see people swimming from underneath.

On the first day there I decided to go canoeing. I waited in line then attempted to get in mine. I got one foot in but it drifted away. I had one foot in the boat and one on the bank and eventually the gap just got too wide and I fell in. I ran all the way back to our chalet with wet clothes and squelchy shoes. Mum had only packed one pair and I had to wait for them to dry out. They used a hair dryer in the end. I couldn't have been much of a holiday for Mum because she did self-catering and, of course, took both milchich and fleishich utensils.

I spent hours riding on the chair lift, but my very favourite time was going to a kids' magic show. The magician wore a black cloak and did the usual tricks, and then asked for a volunteer to help him. I was on the stage in seconds. It was a guillotine trick. First he showed how the guillotine worked and then did it again, chopping a cucumber in half. Then it was my go. I put my head under the blade and he released it. I felt a slight thud on the back of my neck, and then he stood me up to a smattering of applause, but I loved it.

In 1962, we took the ferry, then the train to Paris. We went with a group and I have a picture of us all outside the Gare du Nord. We saw the usual tourist things like the Eiffel Tower and stayed in a small hotel with a dusty square in front where I watched men playing boules. Mum and Dad went out one night and put me in charge of Stephen and Paul. I was fourteen, Stephen was twelve and Paul was six. They wouldn't stop jumping on the bed and making a noise. I gave up. The owner of the hotel came in and complained to us and later to our parents. I found out that they had been to the Moulin Rouge and Mum said Dad was embarrassed by the topless dancers but it was probably her.

I was eleven in 1959 and sat my 11+ exam. I remember the day the letter came saying that I had passed and that I was going to King George V Grammar School on Scarisbrick New Road. I ran round the house whooping. I was a careful boy and as the time to start approached, I decided to do a trial run on my new bike with drop handlebars to "test" the route. We bought it from a bike shop on the bridge near Meols Cop station. It was named "Blue Streak" after a British rocket that was scrapped in the early 1960s.

There were various school traditions. The only kind of bag allowed was a canvas haversack, decorated with whatever emblems suited you. It had to be grubby as soon as possible. Any kind of briefcase was not cool. The other convention was that the first years, the "newts", must wear their school cap.

On the first day at break, already in a bad temper because I had been put in 2a, the lowest first year class, I went out onto the playing fields wearing my new cap, blazer, and short trousers. Three older boys soon picked on me, and stole my cap. They threw it from one to the other every time I approached the boy who had it. They were laughing and teasing me. Already in a bad mood, I went up to a random one and punched him on the nose. We began a sort of rolling around fight. Then break was over. I got in late to class, full of grass stains, with a bloody nose and a bit bruised. I was asked if I had been fighting and of course denied it. I was sent to the head, Geoffrey Dixon, who warned me most severely that this kind of behaviour would not be tolerated. He sat there, behind his desk, in his black gown, on his moral high ground, wasting his precious time speaking to a lowly new boy and I felt I was a creature from another world.

I soon discovered, however, that the fight had been to my advantage. The story had gone round the school and helped to cement my reputation as someone not to be messed with. Two years later, this incident also helped Stephen. On his first day, several older boys saw him and said, "There's a "newt", let's get him," but another one shouted, "No, leave him alone, he's Geoffrey Windham's brother."

I soon discovered a love for rugby. K.G.V. was a grammar school and played rugby not football. On the very first rugby lesson with "Windy" Gale, the P.E. teacher, I was putting myself about, being the tough guy and soon I became part of the school rugby team. There was a team for each year and a busy schedule. What helped me was that matches were played on Wednesday afternoons as well as Saturdays or I would have been in the same situation as Holy Trinity. I was always played on Wednesdays in both home and away matches. I became one of the jocks and part of a group that had certain privileges like extra wagon wheels and milk at break, not having to queue, and where we could stand about. We felt we deserved respect and arrogantly showed it to lesser mortals.

My rugby regret is that, Edwards, the house I was put into contained none of my rugby friends, in fact we were rubbish. So in the rugby house competitions, no matter how hard I tried, we never won anything. Masons house was the overall best at that time. Some of the other houses were Woodhams, Evans, Grears, and Leeches,

The forms in the first year at KGV were streamed as 2A, 2Y and 2X. X was for "express", the high achievers and they would do their GCEs in one less year. There were thirty boys in each class, in other words the top ninety of the 11+. Those below the top ninety went to the secondary modern, Meols Cop, which was across the fields at the back of KGV. We were warned not to fraternise with them, especially not to talk to the girls.

Being in 2a, the lowest stream, really upset me and I was determined that in the second year I would go into 3Y. In the second year, there was an intake of boys who had passed their 12+, so there were four streams, 3B, 3A, 3Y and 3X. To get into 3Y meant being good at Latin. Latin was majorly boring. It consisted of learning long lists of words and translating passages of Latin into English. The story always seemed to be about some Roman battle and a bridge.

At the end of each week was a test on all the words we were supposed to have learned that week. Well, I didn't learn them; I cheated and used a crib sheet. This meant I did quite well and was near the top in Latin. However, I did terribly in the exam at the end of the year. The teacher called me in and asked me what had happened, and I said I wasn't feeling well, which was accepted and sure enough I went into 3Y. I felt totally justified as I believed I should have been there anyway and the rest of my work was certainly good enough.

In the end it didn't matter. I passed five GCEs and then began doing my A levels. The options were limited. I did English, but they made me do French literature, which I hated, and although I had passed French O level, when the A level teacher insisted on teaching us in French, I could not understand him. I became more and more disillusioned. They also made me do economics which I had not done before. The teacher, Percy Longhurst, was not an economics graduate and just read out of a book. We were supposed to take notes.

I soon got fed up with this and bought the same book. When he asked me why I wasn't taking notes, I told him. This did not go down well at all. It was the last straw, and in 1965, at the age of seventeen, I decided enough was enough and I left school. Not one teacher spoke to me about it. Years later having Maths and

English "O" Level did help me when I went back into education and eventually to university.

I have fond memories of rugby and the camaraderie of the team. In 1960, we were in the coach on the way to an away game.

One of the boys has a portable record player and he was playing 45s. Then I heard Buddy Holly singing, "I'm Gonna Love You Too". The opening guitar piece just did something to me. I jumped up, ran over to him and said "What the fuck is that?" I was infected with the Rockin' Pneumonia and the Boogie Woogie Flu and never recovered.

I also got bitten by science fiction after reading "The Death Rays of Ardilla" by W.E. Johns the creator of Biggles. I was a member of the Children's Book Club which sent me a new book every month. I remember the lurid cover more than the story. It opened the way to my reading Superman comics where I learned about time travel, light speed and other dimensions. For example a character called Mr. Mxysptlk, described as an imp from the 5th dimension and Superman time travelling into the past by flying anti-clockwise around the earth faster than the speed of light.

Later I read Isaac Asimov, JG Ballard, Kurt Vonnegut, Arthur C Clarke and others. The two books that influenced me most were Robert A Heinlein's "Stranger in a Strange Land" and Daniel Keye's "Flowers for Algernon". They really were mind expanding.

The most memorable away game we played was against Stoneyhurst College, near Clitheroe in Lancashire. It was a posh Jesuit boarding school in a Grade 1 listed building on a large estate, with many outbuildings. They usually played other Catholic colleges. The place was huge. The coach took us down a long drive and parked in front of the main building. It was built in the late 16th century. We were taken to the changing rooms where we each had our own separate cubicle. On the way we passed an indoor football ground with an earth floor. The rugby pitch was surrounded on all sides by green rolling hills but the game, which we won, was the dirtiest I have ever been involved in. Kicking, stamping and gouging seemed to be the norm. We didn't like them, and they didn't like us.

Afterwards we showered, changed and then had a fantastic tea with scones, jam, bread and butter, cakes and cream in huge, old-fashioned, wooden dining room with a roaring log fire. It was a freezing day in the north. We never played them again. The next week we played a team in Wigan. The pitch was in the middle of a run-down estate, the changing rooms were in a shed with a corrugated roof, and after the game we washed in a bucket of cold water. There was no tea or roaring fire. It was a good game though.

The teaching at KGV was not good. The young teachers were Oxbridge graduates with no teacher training or experience. The older ones were totally set in their ways, just like the school. Tight drain pipe trousers were in fashion, but we had to be able to take off our trousers over our shoes. Hair had to be short. If it touched your collar it was too long. Many teachers were sadistic. We were hit with all manner of implements. One of the chemistry teachers used Bunsen burner tubing, others used sticks or the bottom of plimsoles, the precursor to trainers. Blackboard rubbers were thrown at us, and a teacher who taught French and German, nearly strangled me once by tightening my tie. I was gasping, "Please sir, I can't breathe, you're strangling me!" but he didn't stop right away. "Danny" Parsons, the geography teacher, hit us on the head with the long wooden pole that opened the top windows.

Most of them had nicknames. There was Big Taff, Middle Taff and Little Taff, all were Evans. There was "Rubberneck" Harry Smith, who had a really long neck, and Mr C.F. Flemming, called "Cough and Spit", shortened to "Cough", Mr L.C. "Elsie" Hargreaves, "Fanny" Abrams, "Pegleg" George Wakefield whose leg was injured in the war, Harrison the art teacher with his pullover and beard, "Tufty" Jones who was bald except for one tuft, Molotov, because he looked Russian, "Blod" Davis, a Welshman who tried to teach me Latin.

These masters and boys were so much a part of my life, and the day I walked out they were all gone. School, rugby, blues and rock 'n' roll, had been one part of my dual life. The other was shul, cheder, family, and general Jewishness.

What is it about religions that I dislike? Sometimes I am asked if I still believe in God. I do not know what to answer. It is such a loaded question. It sounds like a yes or no would do but it is belief itself that I have a problem with. Belief in God separates and divides us; it does not bring us together.

There is no discussion with someone who believes in God, they are just right. Acting on God's behalf bestows the right to do anything in his name. At least some of the "radical" Muslims are honest. They are open about how wrong those who do not believe are, and their stated intention is to destroy us and our way of life. Other religious leaders profess to be ecumenical and accept that others have different beliefs but, for example, as a Jew, Catholics still believe I am doomed to hell.

I do not believe in God but there is a something that is not a thing that is not dependant on anything to be, including if I believe in it or not. It is not within the realm of thought or feeling. It is not definable, especially by a partial, localised creature like me, and anything I say about it is not it. It is what allows this all to be, and anything that can happen is allowed and does. It is not personal although there is no escape from it.

I can have a personal relationship with it but having no preferences, it does not care what my experience of life is. A God that takes sides and can be offended or pleased is the most dangerous superstition and yet seems to be a fundamental tenet of religion.

Chapter Eight

Music and Romance

Another religious person, a mentor who had a big influence on my life, even though our time together was short, was Chazan Philip Copperman. He became chazzan (shul singer) at Southport in 1955, but I knew him from 1958 to 1959 before he moved on to Glasgow. He had a lovely voice called a "Bel Canto Tenor". He was married to Blossom, who he met in Leeds. When I knew him he was only twenty seven and absolutely passionate about music, both religious and operatic.

Mum was musical and so was the Weinstein side of the family. Uncle Phil played harmonica and Uncle Sam vamped on the piano. Vamping is an old fashioned way of playing simple repetitive chord patterns. Copperman decided the shul needed a choir, and I auditioned. I had a high soprano voice and I loved singing the Jewish melodies. I got the job as lead soprano and first thing I learned was that we were expected to rehearse regularly and not just turn up on the day.

There were about six or so of us. "Shep" Kaitiff, who seemed like an old man to me then, was the bass. He had a brother called "Yank" and his sister, Kitty, was married to Moishe Glazier. Sometimes we would practise in shul and sometimes at Rev. Copperman's. They lived in an old rambling house and Blossom would make us tea and kichels. When I got to know them better I would go round to visit and he would play operatic records and sing for me. I felt very honoured. It was very different from my later forays into rhythm and blues.

There was a choir balcony in shul, but he insisted we sing with him on the bimah. We were his backing group and I learned about harmony, performance, discipline and the joys of singing a phrase over and over until it was right. Unfortunately, this discipline did not transfer into my academic world but it came back when I began to learn the guitar when I was seventeen. We wore black cassocks and when we sang in a packed shul on the yontavim, I felt part of something much bigger than me, something transcendental.

The incident I remember best was on Kol Nidre night, the evening before Yom Kippur, the Day of Atonement. The service is particularly moving and the melody to the main prayer is lovely. We had practised for weeks, but on the evening I arrived late. I ran around to the back entrance of the shul, let myself into the little musty room where we changed, and put on my cassock. The door led directly into the main shul in the corner by the Aron Hakodesh. I took a breath, adjusted my tallis, and straightened my yarmulke. I could hear the service had begun. I opened the door, gathered all my courage together and swept into the shul. Passing the rows of pews and the men's curious looks, I made my way to the bimah, ascended the stairs and took my place just in time for the choir to begin singing. Looking back, I actually quite enjoyed that dramatic entrance.

When Copperman left the town I lost contact with him. I was sad to hear that he died in Netanya in Israel in 2010. There are two audios on YouTube of him singing. There were other chazzans, Chazzan Trabinovitch and Mattie Goldstein, who always stood in for free when there was no paid official, but Philip Copperman was the best.

When he moved on, it became obvious that Rev Glazier would teach me my barmitzvah piece. Each week in shul, a portion of the five books of Moses is read out from the hand-written scrolls made of special parchment, which are taken out of the Aron Hakodesh with great ceremony and singing. It is divided so that it takes a year to complete a cycle. The weekly piece is called the Sedra. The end piece of the Sedra is called the Maftir. Then there is another piece tagged on called the Haftorah. You are not allowed to touch the actual scrolls so a Yod is used. This is a silver pointer with a little hand with a pointing finger on the end.

Usually barmitzvah boys just sing the Maftir and Haftorah but due to my Dad's position in the community my brothers and I were expected to do the whole thing. I was already a pupil of Rev Glazier, and I have written about my experiences with him in an earlier book which is reproduced here.

"Up to the age of about fourteen or fifteen, I would go to his house every Friday night after dinner. I remember the dark winter evenings the best. I would arrive wrapped in the cold damp outside, and was instantly greeted by a huge coal fire roaring at me from the grate.

Twelve white candles, in two brass candelabras, were burning on the dining table which was covered with a white tablecloth, an open Bible ready. The temperature must have been over one hundred Fahrenheit. It smelled like the Sabbath, a combination of the fire, the candles, and cinnamon biscuits, ginger cake, sweet red kosher wine and musty tradition.

We would sit at the table while his wife Kitty and her sister, Rae, who lived with them, sat in chintzy armchairs that were too big for them. The material was shiny from use. They would half listen and argue with each other as if I wasn't there. Rev. Glazier would say "Ok, let's learn." We would read that week's portion of the Bible in Hebrew then in English, trying to discover the meaning. This was my first brush with a search for meaning, and the apparent nit picking of words."

My barmitzvah, in January 1961, was a bit disappointing for me. As I said, I had quite a sweet soprano voice but two weeks before my barmitzvah my voice began to break and I could no longer sing consistently. My voice was all over the place. I knew my part well enough and it went fine with no mistakes, but it wasn't how I had imagined, and when reality doesn't match fantasy there is often disappointment. The party itself was a bit crazy. Mum and Dad had decided to hold it at the Birkdale Palace Hotel, in between Palace Road and Westcliffe Road. It was a large Victorian hotel built in 1866. Hollywood stars and celebrities stayed there in the 1940s and 1950s. The "do" was catered by Barney Bloch, the local Jewish caterer, who also owned a kosher hotel with his wife, Betty, on Bath Street. Later on I became friends with Avril and Geoffrey, his two children.

It was an early evening dinner dance in the main ballroom, and as well as family, and some of my Jewish friends, my parents went through their customer list and invited most of them. They pondered long and hard, going over and over their "owing book". They invited about four hundred and seventy five people. Two years later, at Stephen's barmitzvah, they did it all again and invited five hundred and two.

By the time my brother Paul was barmitzvahed, I think they had seen sense. Paul's was an unusual affair. It was a cold February and the shul boiler had broken so the shul was freezing. They moved the service into the Amelan Hall, where there was heat, and that was where Paul had his barmitzvah. The party was a family dinner at Bloch's hotel. The other Jewish hotel in Southport was run by Leslie and Doreen Walsh. The hotel was named "Delrosa", an amalgamation of his name, with his wife and his daughter Rosemary. Later Abe Sawitz and his wife, Monica, opened a kosher B&B.

The chairman at my "do" was Morrie Lewis whose job it was to introduce all the speakers. He was on the top table, where the family sat, with his wife, Hilda. I gave a speech, Dad gave a speech, Rabbi Silverstone gave a speech, Uncle Bernard gave a speech, Izzy Black, a friend of my Grandparents, gave a speech. There were a lot of speeches.

First there was a reception of smoked salmon and chopped herring, on crackers, and fish balls and picklemeat, crisps and nuts. There was kosher wine and whiskey, a free bar. Then we had a chicken dinner, and after bentsching, (saying grace after meals), led by Rev Glazier, dancing.

I had to start the dancing with Mum. We had decided the easiest was a waltz. I had been having waltz lessons at a dance school over the garage on Mornington Road. It is still there. There were about a dozen of us and we stumbled around the dance floor, our shoes echoing and clomping on the wooden floor, it was quite a racket. The teacher tried to keep us in time by shouting out, "One, two three. One two, three." but I never really got the hang of it.

Actually, I didn't really want to. I just about managed a minute or two with my Mum before thankfully others got up to dance and saved me from my public humiliation. I got some weird presents, a few Jewish prayer books from the more religious guests, about forty travel clocks, a few watches, about thirty low range cameras and money. I didn't want most of the presents and my parents sold a lot of them and took the money to put against the cost of the do. I kept a travel clock by my bed and one camera.

In the summer of 1961, I began going to the Amelan youth club on Sunday evenings. It was above the Amelan Hall at the back of the shul, next to the cheder. The room also doubled as a ceremony room for the two Jewish Masonic lodges. It had a table tennis table and a half-size snooker table. There was a record player and a small supply of scratched 45s. The record I remember being played the most was "Oh Carol", by Neil Sedaka and the B side "One Way Ticket to the Blues".

I had heard a little rock 'n' roll and pop music on the radio, which was not often played, but it was the first time I had heard it in that context. It was a bit of a mystery to me, but as part of the package of the teenage world that was beckoning to me it was very attractive.

I would go with Colin Michaels and sit at the bar where there was a proper Italian coffee machine, and drink my first cappuccinos. I had to hide the fact that I did not know how to pronounce this strange word or to discover it was Italian. We were not allowed to operate the machine; it was always done by a volunteer adult.

Many of the other kids were a few years older than me, and to me, they were also much cooler. The boys wore slacks, open neck shirts and loafers. My Mum was still buying most of my clothes and shoes and I realised that now I wanted a say in what I wore. The other big thing was they could dance. I had never danced with a girl. I used to surreptitiously watch them to try to learn how to be and how to act. I wanted to be like those older kids, who were for the most part, although I didn't know it yet, from affluent families and very middle class.

In late 1962, we had moved house from Hill Street to a detached four bedroom house on Saunders Street, a big step up for all of us. It had a garden at the front and a small drive up to a detached garage at the side. There was a ground floor cellar. At the front were steps leading up to a vestibule, into a hall with a Vernon Ward print of seagulls flying over a stormy sea on the wall. On the left was a room my Dad mostly used, then the room where we ate leading to a kitchen with two sinks and a walk-in larder. There were covered back steps into the garden. On the right was a knocked-through lounge with a plush red sofa and seats, a shiny brown dining table and chairs and a bar.

We each had our own bedroom. There was still no central heating but gas fires and we eventually bought storage heaters. Dad had also moved his butcher shop to larger premises on Bold Street with a plan to modernise. He bought freezers and refrigerated counters, an electric scale and an electric till.

In that year a branch of the Jewish Lads Brigade was formed and Stephen and I joined. I was funny about the material I liked next to my skin, as was Stephen. I couldn't stand anything "rough". Long sleeved wool cardigans were anathema to me, as were labels and seams. The uniforms for the boys were made out of what was to me rough material, but the officer's material was much softer, so my Mum ordered private's uniforms in officer's material. I enjoyed the conformity for a while. I had a great time at the JLB camp in Deal that year. There were hundreds of us under canvas and there was a gale the first night and our tent blew away. Lawrence Berg was in the tent with me.

The next day we caught the ferry to Calais. It was still bad weather, and a terrible crossing. Everyone was throwing up and walkways were slippery with sick. But being boys we recovered quickly once we arrived in France. We marched through Calais with all the other contingents from around the UK. It was great marching to the music of a brass band in front of us.

A strange little occurrence was the Shalosh Seudas. This is a tradition about having a third meal on Shabbos and some adults must have got together and decided this was a good idea to attract youth onto shul premises. So on Saturday afternoons in the Amelan Hall a buffet style late lunch was laid on and I began to go as well as several other girls and boys of my age.

After a few weeks someone suggested making it more interesting by playing spin the bottle with mandatory kissing of whoever won. We played it in the kitchen and the kissing was done in private. This went on for several weeks and I have to say it was the best part of the afternoon, being one of my earliest erotic experiences. No adults were present; they must have gone after preparing the food. Well one afternoon an adult turned up, found out what we were doing and the whole thing was stopped, much to my chagrin. Nobody ever mentioned it again, not to me anyway.

The same year, Colin and I were sitting at the bar, sipping our coffees, when he asked me if I would like to take some girls out. I asked him who. He said there were two Carols who were friends, Carol Bloch and Carole Sylvester. He said he liked Carol Bloch and I would have the other one. I only knew the girls by sight, but I figured that if he wanted Carol Bloch then there must be something better about her, so I said that I would, but that we should toss a coin to see which Carol we would get. He agreed and we tossed the coin. He won, and chose Carol Bloch. So that is how I came to go out with my future wife.

The plan was that Colin and I would ring and make the date for the next Saturday night and take them to the pictures. I decided that I couldn't ring from home because it was important to me to keep it secret from my Mum, so I phoned from a phone box at the end of Lord Street near Sandown Court. It was the old button A and button B type. The phone rang and Joy, Carole's older sister, answered. I said who I was and asked if I could speak to Carole. Joy shouted,

"Carole, Geoffrey's on the phone!"

And I heard the sound of Carole thundering down the stairs. I found out later that she knew I was going to call. It had been on the girlie telegraph. I said,

"Would you like to go to the pictures on Saturday night?"

Oh yes," she said, "What are we going to see?"

Well, I hadn't thought of that. So I said,

"Something at the Odeon if you like."

And so we arranged to meet outside the Odeon at 7.30.

I don't remember watching the film at all, but that didn't matter. The four of us sat on the back row. At that time Dad had taken to going to the pictures on his own several times a week. He liked going out and later he would travel down to London to see shows, sometimes with my brothers, sometimes with Mum. He always stayed at The Regent Palace Hotel, near Oxford Circus. About halfway through the film I saw Dad's silhouette, complete with his favourite homburg hat, moving across the screen as he walked from one side of the cinema to the other. We slid down in our seats, but luckily he didn't see us.

We were both a bit shy and after a few dates when I didn't even hold her hand, Carole hatched a plan with Joy. The idea was that when we were out walking she would pretend to slip and nearly fall and hold onto my hand to save herself. Carole put her plan into action one evening when we were walking home after the pictures. We had just turned onto Hesketh Drive off Roe Lane. I was wearing a short mohair overcoat. She slipped, and we held hands all the way home.

I became braver after that and I remember my first attempt to get my hand down her top. We were in the pictures and I had my arm round her shoulders. I gradually moved my hand but got confused and starting feeling her upper arm. I tried again and eventually touched her nipple. It was a great moment for me. Later we would regularly cuddle in her bedroom when everyone was out.

My friend, Lawrence Berg, would stand guard at the bottom of the stairs so we would not get caught. We were very innocent in those days and I never got further than stroking her breasts and kissing for ages. Once she felt my erection through my trousers and asked me if it had a bone in it.

Colin and Carol Bloch didn't go out for long but my Carole and I seemed to just fit together somehow. She lived with her Dad, Manny, her Mum, Rita and her elder sister, Joy, in Carisbrooke Drive. Jaqui, the eldest sister, had already married and left home.

Manny was born in Bishopsgate in 1911. His parents were Samuel Silverstein, born in 1880 in Russia, and Millie Abrahams born in Poland, Russia in 1880. In 1901 Samuel was a hat machinist but by 1911 he had graduated to be a hat and cap manufacturer in business with his younger brother, Joseph. Samuel had two sisters living with them called Annie and Minnie.

Manny had two older sisters, Betty and Florrie and a younger brother, Maurice. Manny was one of those businessmen who took the train daily to Manchester. He had a wholesale haberdashery warehouse in a cellar near the city centre, selling to market traders.

Rita's parents were Mendel Mehlman, born in 1877 in Galicia, Austria, and Jane Swerling born in 1884 in Bedford. Mendel's parents were Sol Abraham Mehlman born in 1857 in the Ukraine, and Morel Malke Rekler born in 1859 in the Ukraine. Rita, Carole's Mum, was born in 1913 in Islington, and she married Manny in Willesden in June 1934. Rita's siblings were Anne, Ben, Goldie, Murray, Doris born 1919, died 1920, and Stella born 1921 who died from an accident in 1924. We only just found out about Doris and Stella, nobody had ever mentioned them to us.

By 1963, Carole and I became established boyfriend and girlfriend. We went out to the pictures and concerts and house parties in Southport and sometimes to Liverpool on the train. The group we hung about with grew and grew. I remember a party at Carol Bloch's house on Carlisle Road where a dozen or so of us danced the Loco-Motion in the back garden.

We had favourite places to hang out in Southport. The usual meeting place was the Monument on Lord Street. A lot of buses stopped there. Then there was the Sea Bathing Lake we called "The Pool". It was on the front near Pleasureland and held a few thousand people. It was round and the pool was in the centre, with a diving platform at one side. A concrete walkway circled the pool where people sunbathed on towels and then tiered rows of seats most of the way round, rose to another walkway around the top. A cafe was at one end with a large globe of the world on its roof. Coke was sixpence a bottle from a machine. We would sit in the best place for the sun, and look with disdain at the day trippers who were mostly from Liverpool. From 1964 onwards there were dozens of transistors radios all tuned to Radio Caroline playing the latest hits. There was nothing on BBC radio apart from the Top Ten on Sunday with Alan Freeman. Eventually the BBC was forced to start Radio One and poached many of the DJs from the pirates. Unfortunately the pool was demolished in the 80s.

There were two main coffee bars, Sissons on Lord Street and the El Cabalah on Eastbank Street. We called it the "Elc". We would sit for hours with just one cup of cappuccino until we were asked to leave.

It was amazing to be a teenager in the 60s in Southport because we were so close to Liverpool and Manchester. It was like being at the centre of the musical universe. The bands that became so famous after February 1963, when the Beatles single "Please Please Me" was released, followed by the album in March, were the bands that played in the clubs in Southport and at the shul hall dances that we went to in Liverpool.

The Southport groups of the day that I remember were The Teenbeats, The Principles, The Diplomats and Rhythm & Blues Incorporated. The Teenbeats first gig was as The Jets at the Amelan Youth Club in 1960. The drummer with The Principles was Pete Cockhill, nicknamed "Plev" who later married my friend Fran Landsman. Pete is now a well known cranial osteopath and has a centre in Bath. Fran is a documentary film maker and has been a director with the BBC.

The highlight concert of 1963 was the Beatles at the Odeon in Southport. They did a week there in August. I went with Carole and Stephen, and although we had seats near the front, their Vox amps could not compete with the screaming. It was so loud it was impossible to hear anything but it was incredibly exciting to be there. They did play a concert at the Odeon earlier in the year as part of the Helen Shapiro tour. I was going to go but when I found out that Helen Shapiro had been replaced by Gerry and the Pacemakers, I wouldn't buy a ticket. Oh dear.

Carole recalls walking past the Odeon with Carole Bloch and hearing music, they both went in the open doors and hid upstairs in the balcony and watched the Beatles rehearsing.

One of our favourite Southport clubs was the "Ravel Club" which was over a car showroom on Eastbank Street opposite the "Top Hat" which was more of a drinking club. Carole, Stephen and I saw Gene Vincent at the Odeon, on 24th March that year, with

John Leyton, and Jet Harris and Tony Meehan, ex Shadows. There was also the Klik Klik club on Stanley Street which was a bit of a dive.

Carole's Dad was often a bit aggressive. Late one evening I was standing in the doorway, kissing Carole, "snogging" as we called it, and the front door opened, Manny grabbed Carole and without a word pulled her in and slammed the door. Another time there was a dance at the Amelan. Carole should have been home by 10, but it was well after that. The place was packed and we were twisting away, when Manny appeared at the door. He walked right through the crowd and dragged Carole out.

We were good at doing the twist and won a competition. The prize was Bobby Darin's version of Ray Charles's "What'd I Say". Another time there was an outdoor dance on June and Ivan Bennett's farm. The dance competition was judged by the loudness of everybody clapping as each couple crossed from one side of the circle to the other. I walked across in silence and couldn't understand why. I turned around to find I had crossed on my own, Carole had not realised it was our turn.

That summer I went to another Jewish summer school in Felixstowe. Although the Beatles had made their initial impact, the music that was played there was bubble gum stuff like Brian Hyland's "Sealed with a Kiss". "Surf City" by Jan and Dean was also a favourite, which I didn't mind. All the boys would join in with the line, "Two girls for every boy." There was no rock 'n' roll or rhythm and blues that I was into.

The summer went on and Carole and I got closer and closer. We often went on long walks and talked about the future. Then on December 7th 1963, a Saturday, I was in shul sitting with Colin. It was the day that the Beatles were to appear on "Juke Box Jury" a pop show, hosted by David Jacobs. Celebrities would vote "hit or miss" on new releases. There was very little rock 'n' roll or pop music on the TV or the radio in those days, so it was a big deal for us. You either had to buy a record or go to a gig, usually a dance. Then there was a sort of ripple in the congregation, Carole's Mum, Rita, had died. I didn't even know she was ill, and I didn't know what to do.

Eventually, I phoned Carole and we arranged that I would see her at the shiva (week long mourning with prayers) at their house the following night. When I arrived all her relatives were there. Manny was weeping uncontrollably. Carole rushed over to me and we hugged and hugged and she cried. That was when my love for her really deepened. Up until then, although I found her very attractive, it was like a game of love, now it was for real.

Her Aunties, up from London, noticed and they didn't like it. I found out later they determined to split us up. They thought we were too young to be so close, and probably that I was not good enough for her. Mum was pregnant with my sister, Susan, and Manny asked Dad if they would name the new baby after Rita. My sister was born a few days later and one of her Hebrew names is Rivkah, meaning Rebecca, Rita's full name. Carole and I visited my Mum and Susan in the hospital in Liverpool, when Sue was just a few days old.

Frances Landsman's parents, Muriel and Joe, who lived close by on Hesketh Road, took Carole in for a while. They were very kind to her and she gradually recovered a little. I remember going round there and dancing with Carole and Fran to "Do You Love Me" by Brian Poole and the Tremeloes, a cover of the Contours hit. But little did I know there was a plot to take Carole away. By the start of the spring term of 1964, her Auntie Goldie and Uncle Jack had taken her down to London to live with them and sent her to Channing School in Highgate, an exclusive independent school. For her birthday they had arranged for a boy to take her out. She had wanted to go and see the Beatles but they said it was inappropriate and he took her to a variety show at the London Palladium instead, boring.

We wrote to each other for a while but after I addressed a letter to her as Mistress Carole Sylvester, a poor joke on my part, and she asked me not to, and I did it again, she wrote and told me not to write anymore. I was very sad. I thought I would never see her again.

1964 went on, and I decided that I wanted to be a singer in a group. I had always loved singing and by now my voice had settled down. So I enlisted three Jewish boys, who were all a bit younger than me, to start a group I called "The Electrons". John Silverton was on drums, Jonathan Nelson was lead guitar, Clive Myers on rhythm, and David Broudie supposedly on bass, but he really played bass lines on an ordinary guitar. I was the singer.

We practised at John Silverton's house because that was where the drums were. We were not very good but we persevered and actually got some gigs. They were mostly at the Youth Club but sometimes downstairs in the main hall with other groups.

I really got into singing, so when I went to another summer school that year naturally I wanted to sing if I got the chance. It was at Carmel College in Berkshire which was a very expensive private independent school for Jewish boys. A lot of kids from Liverpool were there as well as a large Southport contingent. The place was really quite luxurious.

A concert was held on the last night so I put my name down. I decided I wanted to sing a Bo Diddley song, "You Can't Judge a Book by the Cover." I couldn't play guitar so I talked a boy who could play into accompanying me. He had never heard of the song so I had to teach him by singing the beat as well as the song. We played to a less than appreciative audience and got polite applause. I didn't care though, I loved it.

In the autumn of 1964, The Electrons got a gig at the Glenpark Club downstairs from the Great Wall of China restaurant on Lord Street. It was on a Sunday afternoon and getting dark. I had talked the management into letting us play during the real group's break and we turned up, just with guitars and asked the proper band if we could use their drums and plug into their amps. Very kindly they agreed. I can't recall their name though.

Well the place was packed and everyone was dancing when they were on. They announced their break and everyone sat down, drinking their cokes and cappuccinos and chatting. We plugged in, did a Beatle's cover and a Little Richard song and nobody took any notice at all. We unplugged, the other band started playing again and everyone got up and danced. A girl came up to me and asked if I was ok. She said she hoped my cold got better and that I got my voice back soon. I suppose I had been trying too hard to sound like Little Richard. Eventually the band just broke up.

I travelled more to Liverpool and began dating girls from Southport and Liverpool, who were not Carole. I was sixteen, not enjoying the academic side of school, and looking for a good time. I went to concerts, often with Stephen. We saw the Rolling Stones 16th September 1964, just before their second American tour, at the ABC Theatre in Wigan. The Moody Blues closed the first half. I think the Mojos were on as well.

I began dating a girl in Manchester and we often went to the CIS building in Manchester and saw lots of local bands there as well as Jerry Lee Lewis and Chuck Berry. They were dances not concerts. It was a huge ballroom with a sprung dance floor on the first floor. We danced at the Oasis Club on Lloyd Street and drank coffee at the Mogambo coffee bar on Princess Street. Occasionally George Best was there but it was not cool to go over and talk to him. I took her out until the summer of 1965. I broke up with her by letter, something I am not proud of.

When I went over to Manchester to see her at the weekend, I took the train and stayed with Auntie Vivi and Uncle Bernard at their new house on Bury New Road. Bernard was now a successful vet and had moved there from Kings Road in Prestwich. It was a big house with a drive. The surgery was in the house. Vivi kept the place spotless. Both the waiting room and surgery were bleached each day. I liked staying there and strangely liked the sterilised milk they always drank, especially in a milk-shake. My Grandparents left Elizabeth Street and moved into Vivi and Bernard's old house. There was some kind of arrangement for my Grandparents to pay the mortgage in lieu of rent.

Michael, my cousin, is now ultra frum, a Charedi in Prestwich with over fifty grandchildren, but in those days of Kings Road and later, before he went to university and got radicalised, he was an avid collector of Elvis Presley, Brenda Lee, and Cliff Richard records and was a member of the Cliff fan club. Cliff had aspirations to be a rock 'n' roller then, and I remember Michael playing Cliff's first LP which was covers of songs by Elvis, Jerry Lee, Roy Orbison, Buddy Holly and Gene Vincent, recorded live at Abbey Road Studios. The first time I heard Jerry Lee's "It'll Be Me" was by Cliff in Michael's bedroom at Kings Road.

How I got caught up in my life. I changed the daily events by moving from school to work and in so doing new routines were installed but I was still the same mostly selfish boy I had always been. In the sixties, there was a feeling that the world was gradually becoming a better place, a place where there would be enough for all. Sure there was Vietnam and the Cold War and in school we had practiced hiding under our desks if an atom bomb was dropped and told to line the windows with newspaper to protect against radiation, but I was a child of the times, just another fledging consumer. Peace and love became another slogan.

I didn't know that the options presented to me as choices were severely limited. I, along with my generation, was sold the lie that if you worked hard enough and wanted something enough then eventually you would reap your reward, but every winner is supported by countless losers, every saint is raised up on the backs of the fallen, every prize built on the broken hearts of the disappointed. If life is about winning and never showing yourself up, love becomes just another prize.

Chapter Nine

Life in the World of Work

In the spring of 1965, I was seventeen, and I left KGV during my "A" level year, and went to work with Dad in his kosher butcher shop in Bold Street. I had helped out before, usually with bad grace, on a Sunday morning, but full time was very different. Each day was prescribed down to the last minute. This was probably Dad's German-ness and has certainly come out in me, although at the time I resisted what I saw as over fussiness. There was a lot to learn.

Monday was preparation day and there were few customers. Dad pickled his own meat in wooden barrels. They were put in the big walk-in fridge over the weekend and on Monday we would carry them out and check how the process was progressing. He wanted to see a balanced pickle all the way through with a colour change to a brighter red. He used salt, saltpetre and whole pickling spice. It was mainly brisket, a cut from the lower chest of the bullock.

We would make our own pickled pressed brisket, usually twice a week. We had a gas cooker in the back of the shop and a large pan with a lid. The brisket was put in with water, with more pickling spice and a cow's foot, which was actually the lower leg. This makes jelly, and when the meat was cooked, and laid in the press some of the gravy was poured on, for taste and for a jelly to form. We also pickled, cooked and pressed beef tongue. The only difference was the shape of the press, which was round.

In the early afternoon one of the butchers would drive the van to the abattoir to collect our weekly supply of beef and lamb. Glazier was the shochet and after he had killed the animal it was also his job to examine the lungs and organs to check for any disease that would make the animal treif and unfit for Jewish consumption. There were also government inspectors who would stamp the animal once they had passed it.

Although Jews are allowed to eat the whole animal, the tradition in England was, and still is, to only eat the forequarter and offal. The meat would be unloaded into the shop, then boned and each cut would be "trabored", which means taking or "digging out" the major veins and arteries. Jews must not consume blood. Certain fat, like the fat around the kidneys, is also not allowed. I think it is forbidden because it was used as a sacrifice to God in the Temple in Jerusalem.

Tuesday morning was serving a few customers and odd jobs, like mincing enough steak for the day and making sausages. Learning to make sausages was one of my first jobs. First make the mix - mince the meat, add rusk, seasoning and water, mix it all up, and fill the barrel of the sausage machine. We used real lamb intestines or casings in those days, kosher of course. They would come preserved in a bag of kosher salt. Then I had to put on the nozzle, slide on the casing, a bit like a condom, hold the nozzle and turn the handle. It was not easy and would have been a good task on the Generation Game. Once that was mastered it was twisting them into links. In a few months I could do the whole process and make links of different numbers while having a chat. Like everything that is practised well, it becomes automatic and then creative. We also sold Blooms vorsht and viennas as well as the Frohwein's brand, delivered to us by the father and son firm of Rosenthal's from Manchester.

Tuesday afternoon was going to Seddon's to collect the dead and plucked chickens and hens, and then preparing them for sale. Chickens were male and for roasting, and hens were female and for making soup. We worked in the back of the shop with the radio on, chatting about this and that.

One person, eventually me, chopped off the toe nails, tips of wings and the head, and then removed the vein from the neck by a slight cut then a pull. The bird was then given over to the other butchers who would eviscerate it in one go. The liver was separated from the guts which were thrown in a metal dustbin along with the head, and wing tips. The liver, stomach and neck were put in the body cavity and the bird was placed in a flat metal box, which held twelve, ready for sale. This took most of the afternoon.

Wednesday was busier with customers and deliveries. We would get meat out of the fridge, make fresh mince and start making orders for delivery, which had to be finished by 10 before customers starting coming in and we had to serve them.

When I first started one of the butchers did the deliveries but later on we employed a driver by the name of Ben Senior, a retired man, who Dad insisted on calling Mr. Junior. But as I was seventeen and eager to pass my driving test, I would go out with George Whipp and be the driver. He even showed me how to double de-clutch. It was used in the days before synchromesh to change gears smoothly.

I had already taken a few lessons, but doing the deliveries was great training and I passed first time. My Dad also took me out on Southport beach where the sand was flat and hard. The sea rarely came in. He was a good teacher and amazingly we hardly argued.

I took my test in the shop van and afterwards drove back to the shop and parked. I went in and told them my good news. Dad said, "Good, go and pick up twenty chickens from Seddon's." There was no messing about with Dad.

Thursday was the earliest start as it was the main selling day of the week. It was the same format as Wednesdays only busier, non-stop and high speed. Friday was a half day mainly for cleaning. My Dad was obsessive about it. The walk-in fridge was washed from top to bottom, the blocks were scrubbed, the bowls and machinery were washed, and the floors were mopped with bleach. Sunday morning was mainly for picklemeat, vorsht, and sausages.

Lunch was from 1 to 2 but by the time we got home, it was 45 minutes at the most. Mum would have lunch ready on the table and we scoffed it down. Sometimes, if she had had a busy morning, at 5 to 1 she would shout, "Oo 'eck!" and run down to Hobbs', the grocer on the corner of Gordon Street, to buy supplies. Dad ran the shop, but Mum was in charge of all the business side of things. She did the accounts, paid the staff, handled staff PAYE and national insurance, did the budgets, and was in charge of the bank accounts. She did all this as well as run the house, do all the cooking and shopping, handle any small repairs, change light bulbs and fuses, do all the washing and ironing, and bring up four children. She did have a weekly cleaner coming in to help her.

I cut myself a lot in the early days and still have the scars. One Monday afternoon the fresh meat had been delivered and the uncut forequarters were on the blocks. I was alone in the front and the others were all doing something in the back. I was trying to bone a warm shin and I stabbed myself in the thigh. I walked to the back, with the knife sticking in me and said, "I've stabbed myself". I then fainted. They took me to A&E but I only got one stitch as a butcher's knife is quite slim.

It was hard work and long hours in the shop and being an undisciplined teenager I often argued with Dad. Sometimes I got the hump so badly that I would walk out. I would return a few hours later after marching up and down Lord Street, and nothing was ever said. Gradually I learned to appreciate the advantages of being organised, and I am grateful to him for all that he taught me. He was a charitable man which I am sure stemmed from his own tragic losses.

Although many of our customers were wealthy and middle class, some of them were poor and could only afford cheap cuts of meat or very small portions of something. Dad, in his generosity, would put extras into these customer's orders, or when they came in shopping, have a parcel ready made up, over and above what they asked for. He wouldn't discuss it with them. It was all done quietly, with no fuss, so nobody would be shamed and so no-one else knew.

We also had regular professional schnorrers visit us from Manchester. Usually this is a pejorative term but Dad treated them with respect. They came expecting a handout, and would do the rounds of people who they knew would give them something, usually money. Dad not only gave them money but also food. He would sit them down, and make them a picklemeat or vorsht sandwich with pickles and a drink and give them a snack for their journey back. He would banter with them, enquire about their health and generally treat them like a person. These were great lessons in the true meaning of charity.

In 1960, Sam Aran opened a kosher butcher on Union Street opposite Arnold Cohen's tailor shop. Tragically, Sam's daughter, Hazel, died in June 1961. He had to sit shiva for her and so couldn't open his shop. Dad went to him and offered that I would work in his shop for a few days to keep it open. I was only thirteen but everything was prepared for me and I just had to hand things over. Sam was amazed but agreed.

So that week I turned up to our rival's shop and served his customers, some of whom were quite embarrassed to see me there. Stephen remembers me bringing a bag of cash home on the Friday which was his weekly takings. We counted it and my Dad remarked, "Is that all he takes in a week?" There and then he topped it up with his own cash. We passed the money on to Sam and never mentioned it. He was very grateful and the next week in shul he went over to my Dad and thanked him again and said that it was his best weekly takings since he had started. Dad said nothing. That was the kind of man he was, and I loved him for it.

Jean was our secretary. She worked Wednesdays and Thursdays. She presented herself as a timid woman, but she could be tough enough, although she did once cry with frustration at Dad. She sat in a little office to the right of the shop with a sliding door, half wood and half glass. There was a one bar electric fire to keep your feet warm. There was no other heating in the shop. She would call out the orders, item by item, to be made up for delivery, and answer the phone.

On the desktop with all the order books and stationary was a great old phone, a big black thing with a plastic slider on the front base. This could be moved to different positions, the main one to "exchange", one "on hold", one "extension" and one "extension to exchange".

Dad had been friendly with a town councillor and helped him in his election and in return the councillor had arranged with the GPO, the post office, to install an extension at home in Saunders Street for free. So in the daytime, if you wanted to make a call from home, you had to ring through to the shop by winding a handle on a little black box and then someone in the shop would switch it to "extension to exchange". How many times did I have to drive back after forgetting to switch it over?

I ask myself, "Will I ever be free, and who is this "I" that imprisons itself by its insistence on being a set somebody?"

The only freedom is freedom from me with all my indoctrinations, and beliefs and opinions, all my little ways to hide my inauthenticity. Yet it is too easy to denigrate the human condition with all our weaknesses, with all our craziness. Isn't it obvious that we are never logical and that our intuition is flawed? I do not cause myself. I am a random event. I am non-volitional. The usual me identity is dependent on circumstance and the significance it grants itself.

Freedom is to be the mirror that loves its reflections, and the reflections that feel loved can love. I can only love my reflections when I am honest about what kind of mirror I am. Otherwise if I profess to love my reflections it is just another of my profit making schemes.

Sometimes up is down. Sometimes down is up. Sometimes there is fear. Sometimes there is love. What a wonder to be here at all.

Chapter Ten

On and Off and On

In 1964, Bob Dylan released the single "The Times They Are a-Changin'" and for the first time I realised that I wanted to play the guitar, so when Auntie Vivi asked me what I wanted for my birthday in January 1965, I asked her for a guitar. I knew nothing about guitars so when she gave me my present I did not know two quite important things. One, it was right handed and I am left handed. Two, it was a really bad instrument she bought from Woolworth's and the action was so high that when I tried to play chords the ends of my fingers would bleed. But I didn't care; I thought that's what you had to go through to learn. So l bought the sheet music of "The Times They Are a-Changin'" and looked carefully at the little chord boxes that showed you where to put your fingers, and painstakingly strummed away. It was Chazan Copperman's influence.

Once I had learned the basic chords and the basic three chord trick with the relevant minor, it became obvious to me that many modern songs were based on this structure, and miracle of miracles I could play many Buddy Holly songs and strum along to blues numbers. But electrification seemed a long way off, and although I disliked many of the English folk songs, I began to learn more and more. Eventually I found out that some guitars were strung with nylon strings and so I bought myself a "Tatay" Spanish guitar from Aldridge's in town because my friend Julian Desser had one. It was so much easier to play, so much easier on my fingers. We began to practise regularly together.

I teamed up with my friends John Taylor (Taz) who sang and harmonised and Charles Hepworth who became our manager. Taz soon learned to play guitar. He later bought a twelve string acoustic off me that I had bought in Frank Hessey's in Stanley Street, Liverpool, the shop where all the groups bought their gear. Then somehow we persuaded a young French girl from Maghull called Kiki to join us. She could just about play but looked very good and we began getting gigs. We played songs like "All My Trials" and "Three Gypsies Stood at the Castle Gate" and a blues song, "Trouble in Mind". I think most audiences liked us.

We played venues in Southport and Liverpool, including the Pink Parrot (John reminded me about this), The Norris Green Social Club, and the Formby Ice Rink. There was another working men's club whose name I cannot remember we were booked to play. However when we arrived it looked so rough I wouldn't go in. We played at the Bothy Folk Club at the Upsteps Pub on Upper Aughton Road. We opened for the Bothy Folk Group whose singer, I think, was married to one of the Spinners a well known Liverpool folk group. I met Kiki years later and she had become a model and lived in New York.

In 1965, my friends and I began frequenting the Kingsway Casino at one end of the Promenade. Charles' Dad, Sydney Hepworth, knew the owner, John James, and would often get us in. The Beatles had made several appearances there in 1962. It was the first gig that Ringo did with them when Pete Best was ill. We went to gamble and see some of the musical acts that appeared there. Pop acts like Status Quo and Brenda Lee were on in the Starlight Room. We would go late, during the week and sometimes stay until they served breakfast. Amazingly I would get up the next day and go to work. I liked blackjack and even had a favourite position at the table. We didn't gamble for big stakes. The most I lost was £25 which was actually a week's wages.

Then Carole re-appeared. Well the first time I saw her was Easter 1965. She was home for the holidays. I was walking down Lord Street one Saturday and I saw her walking into a shop. She was wearing a mini skirt and fishnet tights. I wanted her more than ever but I panicked, and hid. She came out of the shop and walked away from me, so I ran round the block so I could pretend to just bump into her. It worked, and we had a very stilted conversation.

Next time I saw her was later in 1965. I was driving over the railway bridge on Hesketh Drive with Charles Hepworth and there she was walking home towards Carisbrooke Drive. She looked very different to the last time I had seen her. She was wearing paint splattered Levi jeans and carrying a large, black portfolio. I pulled over and shouted hello. We chatted for a while about nothing, and I asked if we could maybe meet up sometime and she agreed.

Our relationship got a bit vague from then on, we went out sometimes but we were not boyfriend-girlfriend. I remember that we stayed over one night at our mutual friend, Hazel Clyne's, on Marlborough Road. We slept in the same bed. Nothing happened but we acted as if it did although we both kept our underwear on.

When I was delivering in the Carisbrooke Drive area, I would pop in to see her for a while. Carole says she recalls me screeching up to her house and slamming the van brakes on.

Later I found out that she was in Southport because she had finished Channing School and wanted to go to Art College. Uncle Jack, Goldie's husband, had other plans. Amongst other investments, he owned a fashion chain called "Bradmore's". Carole was still living with them and he wanted Carole to train in one of his shops and work her way up. Carole was adamant that she was going to be an artist. Jack said not if you live here, and so she defied him and returned to Southport to live with her Dad and go to Southport Art College.

The next major event that year was seeing Bob Dylan play at the Odeon in Liverpool on May 1st. Some of our group had been going to the Jewish youth club in Liverpool in Dunbabin Road, called Harold House. It was run by Teddy Gold, a social worker. I had seen an advert for the Dylan concert on the notice board. They had obtained a block booking. Well I had to go and I got three tickets, one for me, one for Stephen and one for Sharron Fletcher. We sat on the front row of the balcony with a few dozen other Jewish kids. Stephen reminded me that he started with "Times They Are a-Changing" but the microphone only came on halfway through the song and everybody cheered. Dylan was amazing, and from that moment on Stephen was a major convert. Ever since then when Dylan tours Britain, Stephen goes to nearly every concert. He has all his recordings, including bootlegs, of which there are many, and some of Dylan's art hangs on the wall of his flat.

Later that year Dad bought me a car. It was an Austin A40, second-hand of course. At that time my closest friends were Charles, Taz and Mike. I remember going to a big dance somewhere north of Blackpool on the way to Fleetwood. We went there a few times. I particularly remember dancing to Percy Sledge's "When a Man Loves a Woman".

This particular dance finished quite late and we set off home down the A40. In the middle of nowhere, and in the dark, steam starting pouring out of the engine so I pulled over to the side of the road. We looked under the bonnet and the radiator was dry. Where to get water?

There was a little stream by the side of the road but it was too shallow to get anything out of it. There was what looked like an old farmhouse with lights on across the fields. So we walked over and knocked on the door. An old woman answered and we explained our predicament. She asked us in. The room was lit with a low powered bulb but we could see a middle aged man in the gloom sawing through an upright piano. I gulped, but we were in. He had heard our story. He stopped sawing and got us a container and filled it with water and without saying a word handed it over. We thanked him while backing out and we ran across the field back to the car, spilling most of the water on the way. Thankfully, there was enough left, and we were able to drive back home. We had the car checked out but it was not repairable, and I relied on the shop van from then on.

Every Friday I would clean it out, take off the sign on the side, "D Windham Kosher Butcher" and put an eiderdown in the back ready for the weekend. I used to cram my friends in. No seatbelts of course. There were none in the front either. By then the M6 motorway had been built although it didn't connect to the M1 until 1971, and the connection between the motorways was a nightmare for traffic. However, it meant that we could drive to Birmingham in under an hour and sometimes Mike, Charles, Taz and I would go from a club in Manchester or Preston and on to another in Birmingham at 100mph.

There was no speed limit on the motorways until December 1965 and far less traffic, especially at night. We often went for breakfast at Charnock Richard service station. It was one of the first M6 service stations, opened in 1963.

In the summer of 1965, Dad took Stephen and me to Germany. In the early 60s he would often go off and Mum told us he had flown to Dusseldorf and it was something to do with his family. Piecing it together he was visiting a solicitor who was acting on his behalf to claim reparation for his parent's property in Rodenberg. As far as I know he got very little in the end. Anyway, we flew to Dusseldorf and on to Cologne. The hotel he had booked for us had made a mistake and we had to find another. We stayed at the Hotel Mondial close to Cologne cathedral. We even went to a local dance club together and the English pop group the Fortunes were playing. We chatted with them after the gig.

We caught the train to Kobern and when we showed our tickets to the guard he recognised Dad and invited us to his house for lunch. They talked a lot in German which I did not understand. We went to look at his Grandparent's house and several people who had heard he was there came out to see him. They were all crying.

Dad was very uncomfortable and so we didn't stay long. We walked to the local inn and ordered wine and they gave us a bottle each. We went down to the river, sat on the bank and got a bit drunk. We found the local cemetery but the gate was locked and I climbed over the wall which had barbed wire on it, and tore my trousers. I took photos of my great grandfather Samuel's grave and a man appeared and shouted at us. He wanted to know what we were doing and Dad explained to him and he unlocked the gate so I could get out. We returned that day to Cologne.

We only stayed in Germany a few days. It was beautiful and ancient but not too hard to imagine the horrors that had occurred not so long ago. Was it strange being there? Yes, I was walking in freedom with no fear of arrest for being a Jew, on the same streets that my family had walked, streets where Jews had been assaulted and abused. There were men and women in the shops, on the train, in the hotels, who had been alive in the Nazi era. Some of them had been in the Nazi party, unpunished for what they had done.

I understood why Dad would not speak German at home because as I listened to the conversations around me, it was in a language that was associated for me with Hitler's speeches and the worst kind of prejudice that had resulted in the suffering and murder of millions of Jews, Gypsies, Jehovah's Witnesses, gays, vagrants and the mentally and physically disabled as well as the millions of soldiers and civilians who had been killed and injured. We returned to England and just carried on with our lives here. It was barely mentioned.

In 1966, the van was still my main form of transport. I took Stephen to an all nighter at the Twisted Wheel in Manchester in it. When the club closed we went to Manchester Airport for breakfast. I made him swear not to tell Mum. I also went to London a few times with Charles and Taz. We always cheered when we passed the Watford Gap services and sang a song to the tune of the skiffle song "Cumberland Gap". We usually slept in the van.

On one of those trips I remember waking up and putting the radio on to listen to Paperback Writer the first time it was aired. It was June 10th 1966. That night we decided to sleep at Heathrow Airport on a bench but after a few hours we got thrown out when we couldn't produce a ticket. The three of us also went to the Beatles offices on Baker Street in 1968 As far as I recall we just knocked on the front door and someone let us in. We just wandered around the offices for a while. Most of the rooms were not being used or were not properly furnished, and after a while we just left.

In 1967, Carole and I were still in a sort of not a relationship. I often went out without her and she did the same. I saw Zoot Money and the Big Roll band in a little club in Preston but can't remember who with. I also saw Rory Gallagher at least three times in Liverpool, not a club gig but not seated. He was wild. His guitar was worn back to the wood; his clothes were crumpled denim and his hair shoulder length. He looked and sounded really dangerous to me. What an exciting guitarist and performer.

April and May 1967 were to be great musical months. In April we went to London to stay with Carole's eldest sister, Jacqui. We took her to Alexandra Palace to the "Fourteen Hour Technicolor Dream", a concert and happening in aid of an alternative paper called "The International Times". Loads of big bands played there. I remember watching a John Lennon movie of someone's bottom.

There were hundreds of hippies and the grounds around the building were full of people out of it on dope or tripping on acid. In the crowds inside a girl appeared, took all her clothes off and then two other girls arrived with big tins of paint and painted her all over. It got a big round of applause.

Then there was the Art School Ball. Carole was coming to the end of her course at the Southport Art College. I decided to go but she didn't want to go with me and went on her own. It was at the Moulin Rouge at the Ainsdale end of Southport on May 3rd 1967. The band was Pink Floyd and they did their whole psychedelic set with back projection of oil and water. Carole wore a silver sparkly mini dress. We didn't speak much. Hazel was there as well.

I had just heard about Jimi Hendrix and a few days later I found out he was playing in Manchester. It was at Jimmy Savile's Top Ten Club in the New Elizabethan Ballroom at Belle Vue, May 14th 1967. I asked Carole and Hazel if they would like to see the greatest guitarist in the world. They agreed. I picked them up and Hazel changed from her school uniform in the van when we got there. I had no tickets but the tour was far from a sell-out for some reason and we got in for free. It was a really big ballroom with maybe three hundred people there. Savile did not appear and the band just came on.

Jimi was dressed in all his finery and looked well out of it. He did all his tricks, playing behind his head, and with his teeth. He set fire to his guitar by spraying it with lighter fluid and striking a match. He was mesmerising and we stood right up to the stage, leaning on the edge just a few feet away from him. I have no pictorial record. Now, of course, I would have filmed it all on my phone, but not actually have experienced being there. On the other hand, a video or some pictures would be nice.

In the summer of 1967, Charles, Taz and I went on holiday together to Sitges on the Catalan coast in Spain. We went by train to the south coast, caught a ferry, then through France by train on a third class carriage on wooden seats to Spain. Charles' Dad, Dr. Hepworth, took us to Lime Street Station very early in the morning for the first leg. Everything went well and we made all our connections. When it was getting late that night we realised we had forgotten to book couchettes to sleep on. There was a girl from London in the carriage with us and we took turns sleeping on her. We named her, "The most comfortable girl in the world".

Eventually, we arrived at the hotel and changed into swimsuits and down to the beach. We stayed at the Hotel Cesar, Cami Capellans, advertised as 50 metres from the beach. John just sent me the hotel brochure which he found in his Mum's effects after she died.

In those days we spread olive oil on ourselves to get tanned and the next few days was beach and bar, beach and bar, where we drank far too many "Cuba Libres", a strong version of Bacardi rum and coke, although it probably wasn't Bacardi but some cheap white rum substitute. I used to think that Ron was the first name of the man who invented Bacardi, you know, Ron Bacardi.

On the third day we decided that the best way to pick up some girls was to hire a car. We also hatched a silly plan to drive to Barcelona where Los Bravos, who had just had a hit with "Black is Black", had a studio. I had started writing pop songs and thought that one of them entitled "Lies" would suit their style. We would meet them and sell them the song.

Well that never happened. We hired the car, a little Fiat 500, and we did pick up two girls. They agreed to come for a ride with us, and that evening after having too many Cuba Libres, we headed east out of Sitges and up into the mountains. We intended to go to Barcelona for the evening. I was in the back with the two girls and Charles and Taz were in the front. Well the night was dark, the mountain road was winding and unlit, and we missed a bend and went off the road.

Hitting a tree on the way down broke our fall and we rolled the rest of the way. It was eerie. The engine cut out, but the headlights stayed on, and I could see the ground coming towards us. I was trying to brace myself by stretching out my arms to each side of the car and holding onto something. I thought I was going to die. It was my first major brush with death. Then we stopped. One of the girls was screaming that she had hurt her eye. I put my hand to my back and felt something warm. It was blood, my blood. I felt again and I could feel my spine. I had been cut across the small of my back from side to side. I didn't panic. Maybe I was in shock but there was no pain.

The car was on its side and the others climbed out through the windows, but I could not move my legs. Charles and Taz lifted me out and put me down on the rocky grass. It was dark. Charles said he would go and get help and he and Taz climbed back up to the road and set off.

Eventually they found a farm and got the farmer out of bed. He drove his cattle truck to where we were and they carried me up and laid me in the back. The farmer drove us to a nearby hospital run by nuns. I was stretchered in by them. The nuns removed my clothes and lay me on my front. Some of them poured what felt and smelled like disinfectant on my back while others held me down. I swore a lot. Then a doctor appeared in a summer shirt and shorts. He proceeded to put three stitches in my back, one at each end and one in the middle. They bandaged me up and the next day I was taken back to the hotel.

Although they tried to keep it from me, Charles and Taz and the girl who was not injured were taken into the local police station and given a hard time. The police came the next day anyway, and the girl who had injured her head and I were taken in for questioning.

It was a very hot day and we were taken into a small room with a uniformed policeman. We stood, and he sat behind a desk. It must have been over 100 degrees, and the sweat was beading on me and dripping down my neck. He asked us what had happened and I told him the story we had agreed to, that we had been forced off the road by another car. He laughed at me and got out a gun. Waving it at me he asked me if I wanted us all to go to prison. At this the girl fainted. The policeman seemed exasperated and waved us out. I was taken back to the hotel in a police car and I presume the girl was also returned. I saw her again the next day in hospital when they checked my wound.

The insurance company connected to the car hire firm sent a representative from Barcelona to see us. We met him in a coffee bar near the hotel. I was still all bandaged up and spending most of my time in bed. The firm wanted us to admit liability and pay for the car. We pooled all our money and offered it to him as a bribe which luckily he accepted. He signed some papers that let us off.

The next problem was getting home. We had contacted our holiday insurance and they would not let me go home by train. They said I must fly for medical reasons. They would allow one other to accompany me. Charles volunteered to return alone by train and so Taz would come with me on the plane. We got to the airport and he tried to check us in but they would not allow it. They said I must have a medical certificate certifying I was fit to fly. Taz spent ages arranging it and after waiting for hours, the airport doctor agreed to issue a certificate with minutes to spare.

The plane took off and I realised I was starving but we had no money left. Luckily, the ticket included a meal, but there was no choice and the meal was lamb chops, potatoes and a vegetable. I had never eaten treif meat before, but I looked at the chops and I was so hungry that I ate them. I half expected a lightning bolt to strike the plane and down it, killing us all, and that it would be my fault, but nothing happened. God let me off that day, or maybe he saved it for later. When we arrived at Heathrow, there was an ambulance waiting for me on the tarmac.

My parents had been so worried about me and so relieved to see me that that I was not told off or asked hundreds of questions. I just told them about it in my own time, although I left out the Cuba Libre part. I was examined by my GP and told I was lucky that the wound had healed well. I was taken into the Promenade Hospital and put on a ward where all the other patients had been injured in motor bike accidents. They did what they called a "manipulation" on me, under general anaesthetic, to stretch my spine and alleviate my pain. I was in for two weeks and it took me a while to walk confidently again. Carole visited me but that was the last I saw of her for a while.

Several months later, in the spring of 1968, I was chatting with Mike Marsden, and he said, "Guess what? I know where Carole is, she's in Stoke at College. I've got her address, let's drive down and see her. Until then I had no idea what had happened to her. He told me she was at Flat 9, Park Fields, Park Avenue, Dresden.

So one weekend we set off down the M6 and eventually found a big old house with a leafy garden. The front door was open so we went into a large hall and Carole was in the ground floor flat with several other students. One of them was John Webber who was to become a senior lecturer at the college.

They all seemed very suspicious of us. I knew nothing about art and felt left out of the conversation. But I had met Carole again and I was determined to make a go of it. We stayed a few hours and Carole said it was ok if I visited again. So a few weeks later, I drove down the M6 to Stoke again and Carole and I became closer, although I still did not feel accepted by her friends. They all hung out and drank in pubs and discussed art and philosophy. I was always on the edge of those conversations, an outsider, but I visited more and more.

Then Carole moved into a house-share with a fellow student called Angela Marshall, who later married Ian Byers, another ceramicist. A pattern emerged and most Saturday mornings I left Southport and drove through the night to Stoke. I would often take a piece of brisket or a chicken with me. When I arrived Carole was in bed. I would go into the kitchen, turn the oven on and put it in to roast. Then I would get into bed with her.

It was very old fashioned in Stoke. Pubs still had sawdust on the floor, and we often went to one that was someone's front room with a counter for a bar. I liked the pikelets which were like thick wholemeal pancakes and we bought them from a bakery that sold them over a half-open wooden stable door.

I was still working in Dad's shop, but I was spurred into writing more songs and wondering what to do with them. I was in the Kingsway Casino one weekday night and I saw a local band playing called the Untouchables who I thought were quite good. After their set I went over to talk to them. I asked them if they would be interested in recording a song I had written and I would pay. They were very interested. I contacted a little recording studio on Ashley Road in Altrincham called "Eroica" and booked an afternoon. We rehearsed a few times with me as the singer. The song was called "Hey, Hey, Hey, I'm in Love", and they did a good job.

I only had one song and the contract said we could have a single, so they recorded the Beatles song "No Reply" for the B side. I didn't sing on it and I never saw them after that. I kept the record though and when I went to New York that summer, I took it with me. I had looked up the names of people who might be interested and somehow I found a June Harris, an agent, on 200 West 57th Street.

When I was in New York I contacted her and we met in her offices. She gave me a contact in London called Roy Berry who worked for Campbell Connolly, a publishing firm in Denmark Street. When I returned to England I called him and he agreed to see me. I wrote some more songs to take and Carole said she would come with me.

Dad let me take the day off, and on Friday September 13th 1968, we arrived at his office and I played him my new stuff, which he liked. It was a plush office and he sat behind a large desk, looking very cool, every inch the 60s record dude. He asked Carole if she could sing because he liked our "look" and he could make us in another Sonny and Cher. Unfortunately Carole can't sing. Anyway, he arranged a recording slot for me to do five songs and we signed a contract.

We went down to London again a few weeks later to a little basement recording studio on Denmark Street. I hadn't realised there was going to be a band so I hadn't taken any song sheets with me. There was a drummer, Chris Karan who was really hot stuff, a bass player and rhythm guitarist. I quickly wrote out the lyrics and chords and played the songs to them. They were very experienced session guys and although bored they picked it up very quickly.

Roy called me later and said he was pleased with the songs. A few weeks later his assistant contacted me to say that the group "The Casuals" who had recently had a hit with "Jesamine" were interested in my song, "Saturday Morning Girl", but nothing ever came of it, and I didn't hear from them again.

It was the autumn of 1968 that I got my courage together and asked Carole to marry me. We were sitting outside her flat in Stoke in the maroon Renault 4 that my Dad had bought. When she said yes, I could hardly believe it after all our ups and downs. I was so excited I had to tell someone, so we drove over to Derby that evening to tell Taz and Charles. I've got two addresses for them, 9 Swinbourne Street and 90 Byron Street. I'm not sure which place it was but it was one of the worst dumps I have ever seen. They had no cooker, the electricity was turned off and the walls were damp and peeling.

We arranged an engagement party in Southport at Manny's flat on Lulworth Road. I wrote the text and Taz designed the invitation in late 1960s style lettering.

"Carole and Geoffrey Are Sweethearts

And what A Party There'll Be
Cheese & Wine & A Discotheque
All Starting at 8.30
Carole and Geoffrey Are Sweethearts
July 14th Is The Date
So Dress Up For The Engagement
And Try To Stay Til Late"

In the meantime, I had settled down into working with Dad. I no longer argued with him and I understood not just how to be a hands-on butcher, but also how to run a business. Some of my friends had left Southport to go to college or university. Charles was doing a photography course somewhere in Derby, Taz, now John all the time, had gone to Southport Art College and Mike was still around. Hazel had left for the Bristol Old Vic. I was getting restless too. Grandpa had died in March 1969 and my Grandma was now alone. His death was sudden from a heart attack. He had always hated being old and saw it as a sign of weakness to give in to it.

There is a special Jewish ritual for a dead body which is very respectful. The person is buried quickly, within a day if possible. There is a voluntary society called "Chevra Kadisha", which means "Holy Friends" who perform the ritual washing and dressing. I was a member in my twenties. These days it is usually done at the cemetery but then it was done at the dead person's home. It can take about an hour. I was there when they came round to my Grandpa's house and when they carried out his coffin with him in it. We stood by the door and watched him go. I didn't really grieve at the time.

So when Manny offered me a job working for him at his haberdashery wholesalers in Manchester, it seemed obvious that I would live with my Grandma in Kings Road. So with much difficulty and some tears, I told Mum and Dad that I needed to try something different. They couldn't really say no. So in the Spring I moved to Manchester.

Working for Manny was not easy. It did mean I didn't have to get up so early or wear waterproof Doc Martins and I could dress casual but smart. The firm was called B. Leon which is Manny's sister Betty's married name. When I arrived, he was in the process of moving from a large basement warehouse that was functional rather than pretty, to a modern open plan showroom. In the basement it was much darker, things were more disorganised and stock was in piled up cardboard boxes and on metal shelves.

The market traders he sold to were used to rummaging around in the basement to find ric-rac ribbon, bias binding, coin metal belts, thin and thick elastic, dozens of different types of YKK zips, buttons of all kinds, and lots of other bits and pieces. They told me privately they preferred it down there. There seemed to be more bargains. Sometimes I would go over to the old place with them, where Manny stored old stock, and they would have a fine old time digging away. They would pay me cash and advise me to put some of it into my own pocket. I would basically hang about until a customer came in and then be polite to them. Manny spent most of the day in his office at one end of the showroom. He was often on the phone to his sister Flo who was his main confidante.

Occasionally, he would take me out buying with him but he was very secretive about it. We would drive out of town to a mill or a factory/warehouse. He drove an old, light blue Citroen that had that amazing suspension. It sort of rose when the engine was turned on. He would always go round the back, someone would appear and they would have an animated conversation that I couldn't hear as I was instructed to stay in the car. After a while the conversation was over and they shook hands.

Sometimes I was asked to load a few boxes in the boot or we later got a delivery to the showrooms. So although I was selling stuff, and taking money I learned nothing about how the business worked.

On a buying day out we would go back to Manchester to one of the kosher snack bars and have a lunch that was far too big. It could be a huge piece of salt beef with mustard in two thick slices of rye bread, or chopped and fried fish with a salad. The portions were enormous, but he was always on a diet and like many dieters he would use sweeteners in his coffee. He insisted on buying Carole's engagement ring for us, but it was not from a retail shop. It was a diamond cluster at a big discount and there was no receipt.

I went on a selling trip to Scotland to get orders, although given the sporadic nature of Manny's deals I knew it would have been difficult to fulfil any orders I managed to get. I drove towards Glasgow and arrived in a small Scottish town on a Sunday evening. I went into the local hotel, took my bag in, booked a room, and asked what they had to eat. They said it was Sunday and the kitchen was closed. I asked for tea and biscuits but no. I asked where the nearest restaurant or pub might be where I could get something to eat, but again no, everything was closed on Sunday. I went to bed hungry. Next day, I had no better luck with getting orders in the local stores I tried.

I drove to Glasgow and booked in another flea pit of a hotel. I couldn't stay in the room it was so awful and so I went into town. There was a dance on at Kelvin Hall in Argyle Street. I went in and danced all night. I remember them playing "Honkey Tonk Women." I did manage a few orders in a department store but as I feared we couldn't fulfil it. It was a long drive home.

Living with Grandma was easy for the most part. She still slept in the back room and I was in the front bedroom just like it was in Elizabeth Street all those years earlier. She missed Grandpa terribly although she did not speak of him much. Sometimes she laid a place for Grandpa at the table or called out his name before she realised. She couldn't fall asleep at night and had to take tablets.

Once I stayed out late with Manny and she was very upset I hadn't let her know and she had made me dinner. It was one of the few times she shouted at me, and I bought her a big tub of mint chocolate chip ice-cream, which was her favourite, to say sorry. She loved her TV wrestling and never missed it. There was Mick McManus, Giant Haystacks, Big Daddy, and Kendo Nagasaki but she liked Jackie Pallo the best.

She still cooked the same food each day. Thursday was fish day, and on Fridays she would make me chopped and fried fish sandwiches, with a good dollop of chrain or salad cream, to take with me for lunch. I caught the 135 from the corner of Kings Road and Bury Old Road into the city centre.

Carole occasionally visited at the weekend. She ostensibly stayed in the middle bedroom but Grandma was knocked out by her pills, so Carole would come in with me. On Saturday, we would go to Old Trafford and watch United. This was the era of Charlton, Law and Best. Sometimes we went to Maine Road to watch City and saw Colin Bell, Mike Summerbee and Francis Lee.

At night we danced in all the clubs to that sweet soul music, like Otis Redding, Marvin Gaye and Sam and Dave. We often went to a club where the DJ was Ugli Ray Teret who was later convicted of sexual assaults. After a while Manny decided he couldn't keep me on and so back I went to Southport and Mum and Dad's. I think his sister Flo advised him to do it for my sake as the business was not growing.

In 1969, I met Kevin Godley of 10cc fame in Stoke. He was doing a media course, and was a year ahead of Carole. We got friendly and talked about music a lot and I often went to his house in Sheepfoot Lane in Manchester. He was working on music with his friend Lol Creme and he would play me demos they had made. He once sent me a reel to reel tape of tracks they had recorded with Giorgio Gormelsky. I'm sorry I didn't keep it. In the summer of 1970, I was in Manchester and I went to his Dad's shop to buy something electrical and he asked me if I had heard Kevin's new record, "I'm a Neanderthal Man" and that they were called Hotlegs. I hadn't, but it soon became a big hit. I didn't see him after that. It felt a bit weird to call him.

In the heat wave of July 1969, Carole, Charles and I drove to St Ives for a holiday and to visit the Troika Pottery. Carole's tutor at Southport College of Art had been Monty Siroto and I knew his mum as she occasionally bought meat from us. Anyway, Monty's brother, Benny, was one of the founders of Troika. It was a very hot week in Cornwall and one day we visited the pottery, met Benny, and had a brief conversation. These days Troika is very collectable. Maybe we should have bought something while we were there.

The big July news was the Apollo 11 moon landing. We were sunbathing on July 20th and in the evening went into a cafe that was right on the beach. We had something to eat there and watched the moon landing on the bar TV. They didn't walk on the moon until early the next morning and by that time we had got bored and gone to bed.

That December, John introduced me to Phil Gray who we met at his friend George's flat near the promenade. It was so small that you had to sidle in sideways to get in. Phil was already an accomplished guitarist and into the blues and we got on almost immediately. He was a student at Southport College of Art as well. He came to Carole's 21st birthday party in January 1970 in Stoke, with Mike, Charles and John. Carole cooked sweet and sour chicken with several kosher chickens from our shop. Soon Phil and I were writing songs together and recording them on my big old reel to reel tape recorder. When we recorded at Phil's house we had to sit John on the other side of the room because his voice was so loud.

Grandma died in the January of 1970. It was less than a year after Grandpa's death. She was staying with us in Southport and became ill and confused. She was taken into the Promenade Hospital but didn't last long. They called us early on the morning of her death but by the time we got there it was too late. She didn't want to live without Grandpa. They didn't live to see Carole and me married, or to meet our daughter, Heidi, but they did know Carole and I am glad of that.

In June 1970, Carole graduated from Stoke and moved in with her Dad in Southport and we were married July 12th. I was already staying in the flat over the butcher shop where we were going to live. It was a one bedroom flat with a tiny kitchen. We furnished it with modern furniture, like a shiny black leather suite from Habitat in Manchester, a trendy red and black reversible Casa Pupo rug, and a round red dining table and chairs from Wayfarers in the arcade.

At the stag-night before the wedding, I had friends over and we got very drunk on whisky. They threw me in a bath of cold water with my clothes on. Stephen came as well as Nigel Harris, Mike, Charles, and John. Eventually I passed out and the next morning I was still asleep somewhere and nobody knew where I was until the last minute. I can't remember where I was! Anyway, I arrived at Saunders Street with just a few hours to go with a terrible hangover and wearing sunglasses.

The wedding was at the shul and the dinner was in the Amelan Hall. Carole looked fantastic in her wedding dress. I wore a grey morning suit and a top hat. We had about 200 people, mostly my parents' guests. Stephen was my best man and my sister, Susan, and Carole's niece, Shelly Winston, were the bridesmaids. Paul didn't have an official role. Charles was there with his then girlfriend Lynne Clyne from London, Taz and Mike were there too. We had a party that night in the flat. Everybody had to wear white. Mike brought Rochelle Goldsmith and they were married later that year.

The rabbi who married us, Michael Alony, who was only twenty four, came to the party and got quite drunk. Many of our friends slept over on the floor and so did he. He woke up late and missed "Shachris" morning prayers. The shul executives were looking for him everywhere. Early the next day Carole and I drove to Ringway airport in Manchester to catch a plane to Tenerife for our honeymoon. Our friends came with us to see us on our way and we all had breakfast in the airport. Mike remembers it was 7s 6d each. It was quite a lot for then. So off we flew into a future and the many adventures that were waiting to be discovered, that I could not know or even guess.

How unbearable it is to think you know yourself, to have yourself all mapped out, to have weighed your value and found yourself wanting. But isn't doing that just another way of being right, of being the hero or anti hero in a story that proves you are justified in whatever part you are playing in your life?

Of course I am not enough. I am partial and dependent, a fragment insisting on being an individual and measuring myself against my concept of being whole. This gap is where desire is born and nurtured and the nature of desire is the antithesis of completion. We have to live in this gap to operate in the world, but there is no love in it.

Some of us think that we must be mean to ourselves to keep us on our toes, to make sure we don't slip. We think we know what we are really like and if we relax for a moment then the worst will happen and that is part of the trap. So what to do? Struggle? Give up? Follow some system, apply some technique or worship the latest guru?

What I have found useful is to practise the impossible. I stalk myself and my Geoffrey act, my well repeated habits and routines, not to improve the show but to be the space in which Geoffreyness arises. My intention is to be honest about what it is that Geoffrey is covering up as he tries to present the Geoffrey that he wants to present to the world, as if the inner part of him is real and the outer just a façade, in the hope of hypnotising others into experiencing me the way I desire to be experienced both positive and negative. Being Geoffrey rather than doing Geoffrey strangely dissipates the shroud of resignation that usually accompanies my self-judgment of "Well that's just what I'm like etc." The emphasis of being must be re-chosen again and again. As it is impossible I mostly fail in my practice, but noticing that my anchor is a little lighter encourages me to keep going.

Chapter Eleven

Settling Down

In the September of 1970, Carole started a one year's teacher's training course at Manchester Polytechnic. She travelled there weekdays by train. Every Friday, for the first few months, I would buy her a bouquet of flowers from Allenscott's over the road, and every Friday morning I would make chicken soup in our tiny kitchen while I was working in the shop downstairs. I loved being married to Carole; it was what I had always hoped for since our early days. We decided not to have a baby straight away so we could be together as a couple.

My parents didn't charge us rent or utilities and my wages were £25 per week so we had a bit of money. I bought a decent stereo record player from Joy Pollack's husband who had a wholesale electrical place in Gordon Street. It was great listening to the way the opening to The Beatles "Here Come the Sun" panned from left to right.

The stairs up from the shop were steep and when friends came round in the evening we would open the window and throw the keys down to them. John Taylor was still around and he was our most frequent visitor. You came in the shop front door, then by the side of the office and turned left through two doors that opened outwards, and up the first flight, then right up the second flight. I painted the walls of the stairs that 1970s orange.

November 23rd, Carole and I, together with Stephen and Fran Landsman went to the Floral Hall to see the American Folk and Blues Festival Tour. We had seen many great bands there over the years including the Ike and Tina Turner Revue, The Kinks, and Manfred Mann, but this was a great show. The line up was Bukka White, Sonny Terry and Brownie McGee, Champion Jack Dupree and the Chicago Blues All Stars which for this tour was Willie Dixon on bass, Lafayette Leake on piano, Clifton James on drums, and Walter "Shaky" Horton on harmonica. They had often played on Chess recordings with Chuck Berry, Bo Diddley, Muddy Waters and other big blues stars.

After the gig we waited for them outside and we all went to the Fox and Goose on Neville Street where we had dinner together.

Stephen got them all to sign his programme. Interestingly Bukka White signed as "Booker".

Carole became a teacher in the summer of 1971 and got a job at Smithills Moor Grammar School in Bolton at £20 a week where she worked until August 1972. We had a yellow mini and she had to learn to drive so she could get to work and we decided I would teach her. One day she was driving down Rotten Row and I got out of the car and beat the roof with frustration. After that she seemed to improve and she passed her test first time.

We continued going out to concerts and clubs. On £45 a week and with no bills we had money to spend and we did. Often we would go to Old Trafford on a Saturday afternoon and go clubbing in Manchester in the evening. A memorable gig in 1970 was Deep Purple at the Free Trade Hall in Manchester. Phil Gray came with us and at the interval we went into the bar and we spoke to Tony Ashton of Ashton, Gardener and Dyke who were the opening act. Deep Purple was the loudest band I had ever heard and I couldn't hear properly for the next three days.

By now we were having Seder Night in Southport, traditionally two nights. Vivi, Bernard and Michael would come over from Manchester for the first night. There wasn't enough room around our dining table and Mum set up an overflow table which Vivi always complained about.

Later on when Carole and I had moved out of the flat and Uncle Phil and Fanny lived there, they would Seder with us. I would pass glasses of cherry brandy under the table to Phil and he would get pretty drunk. We would also have ladies over from the Jewish Rest Home opposite Hesketh Park. I would pick them up and drive them back at the end of the evening. It was a tradition to invite people to Seder.

In the summer of 1971, I went to Germany again; this time with Carole and Charles Hepworth. We visited Kobern and repeated my earlier trip to the local inn where we drank wine. We went on a trip up the Rhine to Rudesheim which is famous for its drinking festivals, bars and long drinking tables. It was a bit strange being there again without Dad. In some ways it felt like a victory for me to be there and to freely walk around, to hire a car, to drink in taverns, to take a boat ride, to stay in hotels, all without being arrested for being a Jew.

Even though some of the buildings had changed or been rebuilt, the country was the same as when I had gone with Dad and, more poignantly for me, the same as in the 30s and 40s when the fascists were in power and controlled everyday life with the compliance of the population. How do these totalitarian leaders take over countries around the world, throughout history, as well as now? Is there something about us that desires to be controlled?

Maybe we need an authority's permission to act out our fears on designated others, and make ourselves feel superior by persecuting those who have been labelled as lower castes, not just by you and me, but officially.

On the 5th August, Carole and I went down to London to see the London Rock 'n' Roll Show outdoors at Wembley Stadium. We stayed at her sister Jacqui's in Highgate. It was a mega show. It was all day and the opening acts were British including an early gig by Roy Wood's Wizzard, and Joe Brown, Billy Fury, Wilko Johnson, and Screaming Lord Sutch with strippers. In the afternoon were Bo Diddley, Bill Haley and Jerry Lee.

Little Richard was the penultimate act and just wouldn't leave the stage until he was booed off. The show was closed by Chuck Berry, one of his best performances. He can be a lazy player but he really played with some passion for a change.

That year we also saw Chuck Berry and the Kinks at the Liverpool Stadium near Exchange Station. The Stadium was actually a boxing venue and the ring in the centre was the stage with the area behind it curtained off on one side. The floor was concrete and the seating was tiered concrete. People would get there early and just hang about outside. It was probably the most run-down dingy venue I have ever been in. The walls were pasted with torn boxing adverts and there was rubbish on the floor. The place had a menacing atmosphere and the toilets were definitely to be avoided, but it fitted well with the dangerous side of rock 'n' roll music. I think it was run by Pete Best's dad.

In the autumn of 1972 Carole and I decided that it was time to get our own place and after much searching we found a big three bed semi in Mallee Crescent in Churchtown, a suburb of Southport. It had a massive back garden and a detached garage. It was £6,750. I put an offer in for it and it was accepted. The back garden was so big it was really unmanageable so that first year the most I did was to mow the grass now and then.

Carole had finished teaching at Bolton in the summer of 1972 and she applied for a job at Southport Art College. By now Phil Gray had left the college and gone on to Epsom so I had no-one to write songs with anymore. Carole started teaching there in September 1973 where she stayed until July 1981. We became friends with some of the staff and remained friends with a few such as Ken Roberts the print maker, who later married an American girl and has been living in New Mexico for many years.

One of Carole's students was Marc Almond. Marc often baby-sat for our daughter Heidi with his friend Hugh Feather, who did some of the graphics of the early albums. Marc was always an outrageous boy. I remember shouting at him for making a long distance phone call at our house while we were out. The last time I saw him was in Leeds where he was at Art College.

I had got into buying and selling vintage items from the 40s and 50s and I used to go up into the Lancashire Hills and around Blackburn and Chorley buying stuff. Sometimes I bought at auctions as well. I began to sell at antique fairs and there was a big one in Leeds at an old railway station. In late 1980, Carole came with me and we were on our stall when Marc came up to say hello. We chatted for a while and he told me that he had a record coming out soon. He seemed very excited by it. I didn't know he was a singer and I said something like "Oh, great", and he wandered off with a promise to keep in touch. Next time I heard of him was when "Tainted Love" was a massive hit. The song really suited him.

I was now properly established in the butcher shop and eager to expand into delicatessen, frozen and prepared foods. I had seen this in America and it wasn't really happening yet in the UK. We even began koshering poultry for customers. Koshering means soaking meat or poultry in water for half an hour, then sprinkling salt on it and leaving it for an hour before washing the salt off again. This is supposed to remove any blood left. We then froze them. It was quite an innovation.

As well as cooked meats, sausages and vorsht, I made sausage rolls, minced meat pies, beef burgers, chopped liver and chopped herring and sold them fresh and frozen. This went really well and I came up with a cunning plan to sell to the Jewish Grocers in Liverpool.

I ordered plastic packets printed with the legend "Windham's Kosher Products" and "Windhamburger", and set off for Liverpool. I went to Wally Levitt's Childwall Kosher Grocers on Woolton Road, Silver's the bakers on Brownlow Hill near town, Chalkin's bakers near the Penny Lane roundabout, and Axelrod's grocery shop on Smithdown Road. I was very confidant and left samples with them all. A week later I phoned them and they all gave me orders. So began a weekly Wednesday afternoon run. After a while my mum decided to take over the delivery. I think she quite enjoyed being on her own out of the house. Years later she told me she would stop for fish and chips on the way home. Stephen and Paul often took the job on in the summer holidays.

Dad and I were probably the closest to each other in the mid 1970s. He got into ten pin bowling and I had bowled a bit with my friends so we decided to join a league at the Litherland Alley in Liverpool. We would drive there together on Thursday evenings. Our main rivals were another father and son team called the Mins, tall thin people, but we never beat them. It was enjoyable for a year or two. We owned our own bowling balls and shoes so we were quite serious about it. Dad was always particular about details and being organised and I am like that too.

There were issues with the grocers in Southport. Julius and Stella Werner ran a shop on Tulketh Street called Makoleth, which means grocery store. They were friends with Mum and Dad for quite a while. Stella and Mum would talk for hours on the phone and they were part of a kalooki playing circle. They had a delivery driver called Clarice. When meat prices went up and meat consumption went down, Dad tried to think of ways to increase our income. There was an agreement between him and a deli on Union Street called "Easy Eats", later taken over by Jack Gaurdi, so they could sell pre-packed kosher chickens and meat and in return we could sell bread. It was sanctioned by the shul and we had daily deliveries of fresh bread from the "Machzikei Hadas" bakery in Manchester. The name means Upholders of the Faith.

The bagels and bread were delivered warm in large paper flour sacks. Unfortunately, it drove a rift between my parents and the Werners and they stopped talking. Dad had already branched into kosher tinned and packaged goods from Mrs Ellswood, Blooms and Hebrew National. We always had a large tin of Jumping Fox sweet and sour pickled cucumbers on the counter.

We also did Pesach orders, first from the empty flat over the shop, and then out of the cellars at Saunders Street. I remember the order boxes piled high full of Paisadicky or Passover products. That means goods sanctioned by the Beth Din to contain no bread at all, even things like toothpaste. We sold hot salt beef on Sunday mornings. I could not each lunch on those far-off salt beef days. We had a portable water heater that kept the salt beef warm. I loved it with pickles and mustard on black bread. I can see my Dad slicing the salt beef on a wooden board now.

In 1973 we decided that we would try for a baby and on Monday 27th May 1974, the first day of Shavuos, at 6.30 pm Heidi was born in the Christiana Hartley Maternity Hospital in Curzon Road. She weighed eight pounds. Although Carole now thinks she may have got her dates wrong, then we thought that she was a week late and so the doctors decided to induce her. So she did not go through the usual build up and went into hospital and straight into full blown labour. In those days it was not standard practice for the father to be there and when I requested this they made me promise that if I felt faint I must leave. Needless to say I was determined to stay.

I remember Heidi being born and seeing the top of her head first with her black hair. Then she was out into the world and I was unable to put my feeling into words, but my heart was bursting. Carole held her then I held her and I kissed them both, and then the nurses took her off to do whatever it is they do with new-borns. We were still in the delivery room and they brought Carole a salad but I ate most of it. Carole was radiant, her eyes were bright and sparkling and she had broken tiny blood vessels in them from the effort. They were like little stars.

After a while I went home and Fran Landsman and Robert Broudie were in the house waiting for me. They stayed to give me love and company and then I went to bed and fell asleep immediately.

So what was it like becoming a daddy? Well hard work of course and sleepless nights, the usual experience for new parents. Carole and I took turns getting up at night. Heidi was not a great sleeper and I would pace up and down her bedroom under the blue sky and white clouds that Carole had painted on her ceiling, singing away until she was asleep. I made up a little story for her about fairies getting their wings wet in the long grass and then the sun drying them out so they could fly again. Sometimes I would lay her in her little carry cot, put her on the back seat of our white mini traveller and drive around until she finally slept. She would lie on her stomach in her carry-cot so she could look around and see what was going on.

Carole had still been painting Heid's room the week before Heidi's birth. She was fifty four inches around the waist but up and down the ladder she went. We went to the Floral Hall on April 5th to see Roxy Music. We had convinced ourselves over the years that it was the week before the birth but when I looked it up I found we had romanticised our memories. She was still pretty big though. We gave Heidi the Hebrew/Yiddish name of Rivka Tsivyah after Carole's Mum and my Grandma. It wasn't until much later that I realised that her initials "H.W." were the same as my Dad's German name.

Loving your child is a very special kind of love. It's unselfish and it seemed to me the most natural thing in the world to put her needs before my own. I had been a very selfish person until then. I know some people struggle with this, but for me it just happened, although I still got tired and irritable. I'm not saying I was able to completely reduce my self-importance, that great waster of energy, but the possibility opened up without me realising it.

Carole took some maternity leave and then continued teaching part-time, Mum was fantastic and baby-sat Heidi so Carole could work. Then Heidi started at the Emmanuel Road Play School on the corner of Cambridge Road. Mum would take and collect her. She stayed at Saunders Street until Carole had finished work.

Meanwhile Moishe Glazier's health was deteriorating. He had retired a few years earlier but still came into the shop to do some traboring for us. However it became obvious he had what I now know as dementia and it became too dangerous to let him have a knife. It was a sad decline. He did visit us with Kitty in Mallee Crescent and he saw Heids in her cot, but he died on the 24th March 1975. He had been a pivotal figure in my life.

With Glazier's retirement we still needed to have a meat and poultry supply and we arranged with the Liverpool Shechita Board to have our meat killed in Liverpool and supplied by Pollock's, the Jewish wholesalers who would deliver it to us. Poultry was more problematic. We contacted the Manchester Beth Din who gave us permission to use some of their shochets. The Seddons retired around the same time and so we had to find new poultry wholesalers.

We first went to a wholesaler on the road to Ormskirk, just outside Southport but that didn't last long. It became my job to ferry the shochet over from Manchester and back again. That often meant staying over with them. They were ultra-frum and the shochet I remember best had a photo of Rabbi Schneerson on the wall who was the last "Lubavitcher Rebbe", often referred to as the "Rebbe". There are many books and articles about him. Some even thought of him as the Messiah. Anyway, I would have to pray with them. I felt quite inadequate in my Jewishness when I was around them.

A little earlier than this, there had been an outbreak of avian flu and Seddons were unable to get a supply. Dad sent me up into the Lancashire hills to find a farmer willing to sell me some. I had the foresight to take some wooden crates and a hanging scale with me. Eventually after being turned away several times I found a farmer who agreed to sell me sixty hens. The catch was that I had to gather them myself. He took me to the barn where they were and left me to it. The technique was to catch six by the legs, then tie a rope loop knot around their legs, weigh them and put them in the crate.

The crates were wooden with a little hatch on top. They didn't want to be caught, they didn't want to be tied, they didn't want to be weighed and they didn't want to go in the crate. It took me over an hour, but I did it and returned home in triumph.

The next place we found was Marsh's in Tarleton, out in the country towards Preston. They were one of the first to raise poultry in massive sheds and men from the ministry of agriculture were often there. The owner was Tom Marsh, a very tall man with a laconic style. I think he is dead now and the business is run by his son. He wasn't interested at first, as the numbers we required were comparatively very small, but now they are now one of the biggest suppliers of kosher poultry in the North.

One day, I arrived to pick up our order and I found Tom in a field with a horse giving birth. He shouted me over to come and help. The foal's forelegs had been born but it was stuck. He tied rope around its legs and then stuck his hand into the mother after dipping it into a bucket of soapy water to act as a lubricant. He then instructed me to get hold of the rope and we both pulled and pulled. After a few minutes the foal suddenly popped out and we both fell over. What a wonderful moment.

That year I was involved in a car accident which was completely my fault. I was delivering to Liverpool and coming through Thornton. I had stopped at the lights before turning left. As I was the first at the lights there was no traffic in front of me. I turned and saw what I thought was moving traffic about three of four hundred yards ahead. My mistake, they were stationary, waiting at temporary lights. I realised too late and drove into the queue, and hit a motorbike.

Luckily the driver was not injured but the police prosecuted me and I was in danger of losing my licence. We went to see our solicitor, Noel Adler, who agreed to represent me in court. He told me that he was going to argue that, as the kosher butcher, losing my licence would be detrimental to the Jewish community. He said that in court he would put questions to me, but that I should not look at him when I answered but at the magistrate. So the day of the court came, I put on my best suit and tie and did as I was told. I got fined but kept my licence. Oh the power of a good solicitor using the race card.

In the May of 1975, we flew to Milano Marittima, a seaside resort on the Ravenna area of Italy on the Adriatic coast. We went with Karen and Mike Rappaport and one of their two daughters Amy and Penny. I'm not sure if they were both born then. We were introduced to them through David Toubkin, and we often visited each other's houses. Heidi turned one in Italy and the hotel made her a birthday cake. It was memorable for Heidi's first proper steps. She walked right across the marble floor of the hotel foyer. We all cheered.

My Mum and Dad were not sophisticated people and I was a naive boy and a naive teenager. I wasn't taught the art of talking people into things. The morality they taught me included living a good Jewish life, being honest in my dealing with others, doing my best, not showing myself up, and keeping safe. The safety agenda was one of the most difficult to deal with as a teenager. When I went out Mum would stay up no matter how late I came home. As I parked and walked up the steps to our house I could see the front room curtains twitching. By the time I got in she was upstairs in bed. The other big rule was not to upset Dad as he had been upset enough in his life. I wasn't too successful at that.

These days using language to fool others and defend ourselves from being shown up is familiar to us all. Double-speak language is in common usage like "collateral damage" or "patient/student/customer centred", and useless concept phrases like "blue sky thinking" and "singing from the same hymn-sheet", hide a poverty of authenticity that is forbidden to be publically named. We all seem to be on some kind of journey now and apparently we all agree how important it is to know yourself and how you must love yourself before you can love others. I object to these ideas and others like them because they seem to be beyond questioning, a new orthodoxy.

Speaking the language of propaganda eventually makes a lie believable, and we have learned to speak a duplicitous language to appear acceptable in our social, work and spiritual realms. Maybe if I had learned how to win friends and influence others earlier, I would have been more materially successful in the world.

I service my body daily. I feed its preferences with food and sex and clothes and toys and entertainment and things to ease my life. It is a never ending task. This is one of the functions of the me-monologue in my head that pretends to be a conversation. It stock-takes itself in the form of my beliefs and opinions and tries to make the events of my life fit with the meanings I have inherited and adapted.

Chapter Twelve

Catering

Barney Bloch, the kosher caterer and Southport hotelier, died in 1976. By this time I had become part of the Chevra Kadisha or Holy Friends. Here is an extract from my book "Usual Me",

"The Chevra Kadisha was the burial society, a small number of men that could be called on to perform the Jewish ritual of cleaning and dressing the dead body.

Rev Glazier had invited me to join this exclusive group. He said to come along, to stay near the door and if I didn't like it, to leave and no-one would mention it again. I agreed, not really knowing what I was agreeing to, but I was young.

One evening I got a phone call. Can you be at the cemetery at 7.30? So with fear in my heart, and morbid curiosity driving me, I went to the cemetery. It was perfect evening for my initiation. Everything was covered in new snow that shone and sparkled with a yellow hue from the street lights.

The night was still and the rows of gravestones stood like black dominos sprinkled with stardust, dark shadows angling across them. I knew someone has already arrived because of the footprints that made a path for me to a little part brick house that stood at one end. I walked the path treading in the footprints as I went. I knocked. Later, when I was more experienced, I would just walk in.

Moishe Glazier was there, as was Sydney Galkoff who took over leadership when Glazier retired, but my eyes were irresistibly focused on the raised marble slab in the centre of the room. On the slab was a body wrapped in a white sheet. There was a small heater blowing in the corner.

My hand was shaken by each man as they arrived. There was also a direct look into my eyes. I felt frightened, excited, and expectant. My mouth was dry. I was light-headed. There was a slight buzzing in my ears. I could not concentrate on what people were saying to me.

All that mattered was that I was in the presence of death. There was a reverential, respectful, feel to the room. I was in an altered state, the first of many. I was a witness that first night, as every night I was there, a witness to the finality of death.

There was no doubt in my mind that the man who lay on the slab was dead. I could feel there was something missing. I knew from that moment on that Geoffrey was temporary on this Earth. This is something I forget a lot. "

I mention this partly because I was one of the men that performed the ritual for Barney. He had been a larger than life man and now there he was. I had known all the men and boys who were laid on that slab, but I had many dealings with him over the years and it was especially moving for all us of there that evening.

One day Rabbi Alony and Sydney Galkoff, who was an ex Liverpool kosher butcher, the head of the Southport Kashrus Commission who collected shechita money from us, and a friend of Dad, came in to the shop looking very serious. Dad was not in. I should explain that shechita money was a tax we had to pay to the Southport shul on the meat and poultry we sold. They did absolutely nothing in return as far as I was concerned. We passed part of the tax onto our customers which meant that already expensive meat was even dearer.

Rabbi Alony told me that we had to stop supplying the Liverpool and Leeds grocers by order of the Manchester Beth Din. I had used the same tactics as in Liverpool and now had a weekly run across the newly opened M62 motorway to Leeds. We were supplying three shops there. When I argued with him he told me that he was the Rabbi and we must do as he said. Sydney didn't say anything. I think he was embarrassed. So we had to give up part of our business which I had so carefully nurtured. It was to do with money of course. The all-powerful Manchester Beth Din was making nothing out of our sales as we did not pay for a hechsher, a seal of approval, from them. Officially, they could do nothing, but they exerted their considerable influence on Rabbi Alony and he had to go along for the sake of his own career.

So I was looking for something else to do and being a kosher caterer seemed like a good idea. I had heard that Geoffrey Bloch had decided to sell his father's catering business. I contacted him and we had several meetings. With Carole's encouragement, I decided to go ahead. He had a chef and a chief waitress they had used for years. She would hire the waitresses who not only waited at table but also cleared up. All the cutlery and plates were washed before and after each event. However, I did not want to take on their chef. I didn't trust him because as far as I could tell he had a drink problem.

I knew the chef at the Jewish Blind Home, Manchester House, opposite Hesketh Park. We supplied them with meat and poultry. His name was Johnny Roseblum and he agreed to be my chef. He was an Auschwitz survivor and had a number tattooed on his arm. He told me he had worked at moving the bodies from the gas chambers to the crematoria. Once he managed to get hold of couple of eggs and hid them in his trousers. As he was walking back to the block where he slept one of the guards kicked him in the balls for fun. The eggs broke and the guards laughed at him because they thought he had shit himself. Many prisoners had chronic diarrhoea.

Bloch's still had some functions booked and Geoffrey suggested I come along and watch what went on in the kitchens. It was very useful. One thing I learned was that, once the do was over, the staff ate the same dinner that had been served to the guests. All the plates and bowls were stored in old wooden beer and pop crates, the really solid ones with cut-out handles and adverts on the side. Then there were the cooking pans, cooking bowls and utensils, fridges, cutlery, trays, tablecloths, napkins etc. etc. Everything was in duplicate for milchich and fleishich. We had enough to feed three hundred people both meat and milk.

I needed premises both for storage and to set up a kitchen with the old fashioned enamelled ovens and burners I had bought as part of the package. I found an empty store room in Ainsdale owned by Stuart Pactor. It was perfect, tall ceiling and large door that opened onto a driveway where the furniture removal van could load and unload. All the stuff was moved there for me by the furniture removers who had worked for Barney for years. They would transport all the equipment to whatever venue and back, sometimes at two or three in the morning. The boss was called Bev. I was all set up.

I began to get bookings, by default at first. People were a bit nervous as they were entrusting their boy's barmitzvah or their daughter's wedding to me. Having Johnny on board was a great help as people knew his cooking and the first wedding I got was because of him. The people were frank that they were booking with me because of him. I was untested.

I learned to discuss menus with my clients, where to buy new equipment, and fruit and vegetables. For tinned goods and packets I went to Makros and local wholesalers. I learned that in most cases whatever price per head we had agreed, the client would try to get a discount when it came to pay the balance, especially if it was a charity do. I learned to make a written contract and to take a non-refundable deposit

The only thing I didn't supply was the bar because I didn't have a licence. I set up a business bank account and I drew out cash on the day so that I could pay the staff in cash after the function was over. I would sit at a table with it and the waitresses and washer-uppers would form a queue and I would pay them one at a time, counting out the money to each of them in turn. The chief waitress got double rates.

The first wedding was at the Amelan Hall and it was a great success. They had opted for a chicken dinner with a simple starter and dessert to cut down on the chances of something going wrong..

I got more functions following my success although the bride and her mother thanked Johnny rather than me. Actually once a function began there was little for me to do. I would just stand by the kitchen door in my tuxedo and watch what was happening in the room. Johnny ran the kitchen and the chief waitress ran the room. Soon I got the contract for the two Jewish Masonic lodges in Southport, Menorah Lodge and Shalom Lodge. They met monthly and then had dinner.

Once we had catered for the lodges a few times Johnny said Carole and I might as well do them ourselves as there were only about fifty people and we could handle it. It was the same menu every time. A grapefruit starter, roast chicken, roast potatoes and peas and then ice cream. Then we started doing day buffet parties. The thing to watch with this is that the client tells you that one hundred people are coming then invites an extra twenty but only pays for one hundred knowing that we would always cater for more. On a sit down do it's easy to count the number of places but on a buffet it is difficult to count the people, so we counted the number of plates put out on the buffet table and charged accordingly.

There were three main venues in Southport where I catered, the Amelan Hall, the Prince of Wales Hotel on Lord Street and the Floral Hall on the Promenade. Apart from that it was in people's homes. The Amelan Hall was the easiest because the kitchens were kosher, but more was involved at the other two. I began to get more orders and probably the busiest week I ever had was in the winter of 1976.

Dad had joined a Masonic lodge in Liverpool. It was half Jews and half police officers a strange combination and sometimes awkwardness was avoided with over the top bonhomie, Dad called it "Hail fellow, well met". I'm not sure why he didn't join a Southport lodge but he talked me into joining too.

It was an interesting experience and my growing discomfort with ritual was sorely tested. I went through all three degrees and learned the Masonic view of God as the Great Architect of the Universe and the story of Hiram Abif, the Masonic guru, the architect of King Solomon's temple in Jerusalem. He was murdered and his body was hidden under an acacia tree. I found the metaphorical resurrection of the third degree, by the light of a single candle, which mimics Hiram being taken up from his grave, the most interesting.

The Liverpool lodge had always used Barney Bloch to cater their Ladies' Night, the big social event in the Masonic calendar. It's basically a dinner and dance honouring the current Worshipful Master, who runs all the ceremonies in the lodge, and his partner. In those days it was always a wife. Now that Barney had died and considering I was a lodge member, they decided to give me the job. It was a roast turkey dinner with all the trimmings at one of the big halls in Liverpool.

That week I had three further bookings. One was a charity do at the Floral Hall, one a barmitzvah to be held at the client's home in Southport, and the other a home do for thirty people. The big ones were for two hundred plus guests. My brother Paul, who often helped us, took charge of the home do. He had two waitresses and a washer-upper.

The Ladies Night was the first. As usual, I arranged the waitresses, ordered the food, and the turkeys. We got massive 30lb ones. The problem was that I had not used the kitchens before and I made the mistake of assuming that would be ok without actually checking. I know, never assume, but I did.

The day arrived and all the food had been delivered. Bev and his mate drove to my kitchens and loaded up their big furniture van like they had done hundreds of times before. We set off for Liverpool in a convoy. We unloaded and for the first time saw the ovens. They were not big enough to get all the turkeys in at once so we started cooking them right away. It became a disaster, the turkeys were just not cooking and we were quickly running out of time. The general panic spread in the kitchen and the eggs for the starter were put on to boil too late. Two hundred eggs are a lot to boil but ordinarily it would be no problem. When it came to peel them, they just wouldn't peel. What a mess.

Well the turkeys never cooked. Mum and Dad were guests and Dad came into the kitchen to try to help. He was very good. I had brought a block of our picklemeat with as an alternative and I had just about enough to serve one slice each. Many tables refused it though. They had waited a long time as we tried to get the turkeys to be ready. A long queue of complaining guests formed at the kitchen door and I had to face some very angry people and stand there and take their insults in public. I apologised a lot. It was the original kitchen nightmare.

We served what we could and the dessert. The dance went on but the atmosphere in the room was oppressive. Eventually they all went home and I paid my staff. They were very supportive, as was Johnny. Mum and Dad thought it was Johnny's fault but I was the boss. I drove home with a heavy heart. Carole was asleep. She remembers half waking as I got into bed and asking me how it went expecting an "Alright". She got a "Terrible". I was exhausted, but still took ages to fall asleep.

The second big do of the week, the charity do, went well, although I knew that if they could have cancelled, they would. They tried extra hard to get a big discount off me, knowing I was in a weakened position but I held firm.

The third do, the barmitzvah went well too. It was a very posh affair in Birkdale. They had a marquee put up in their back garden, not just a little tent but enough to seat two hundred people and accommodate a sprung dance floor. It was a cold December and the marquee was heated and had electric chandeliers. The family was piped in by a pipe band in full Scottish regalia. They had asked for strawberries as part of the dessert. Now in those days soft fruit in England was seasonal and getting a large amount of strawberries was not easy in December. Several suppliers let me down and in the end I contacted a firm in Israel and had them flown in at great cost.

The menu included crepe suzettes, which were cooked individually for each guest at the table, and the dessert was a croquembouche at the centre of each table. I watched Johnny make the profiteroles, inject them with cream, dip them in dark chocolate and pile them into a cone. The whole structure was decorated with caramel sugar threads. Carole was invited as a friend of the family. Once the dancing had begun Carole and I with some friends went quietly into the house and we all got stoned. It had been a long week.

Although I had been a teenager in the 60s, I didn't try any drugs until the 70s and then mostly cannabis. It was just a great way to relax. It was usually block, red Leb or African Black, which was soft and sticky, never grass. We had a weird experience when a friend brought grass back from California in a hollowed out Bible. It was really strong. One evening he came to our flat with a joint ready rolled without telling us it was mixed with heroin. We smoked it and I got tunnel vision and then I was seeing the world as if down the wrong end of a telescope. Then it all turned upside down and I threw up into the toilet. I remember watching the sick in slow motion. Carole said she had a similar experience. We never did that again.

In June 1977 we had a street party for the Queen's jubilee and, like many streets across the country, our street was closed to traffic. On the day we put trestle tables down the centre of the street which was decorated with bunting. The tables were piled high with sandwiches, biscuits, cakes and soft drinks, and there was an unusually friendly atmosphere. The children sat at the tables and the adults went back and forth with food, making sure their kids were ok. Heidi was sure the Queen would come and was really disappointed when she didn't show up.

I had many catering adventures. At one wedding the bride's arrival got later and later. The wedding was at Arnside Road shul and the dinner at the Prince of Wales hotel. It was extra work there as we had to "kosher" the kitchens. All kitchen surfaces had to be scrubbed with boiling water and wrapped in silver foil. Likewise the ovens had to be scoured, left on high for an hour and then lined with foil. We went in through the back and through a maze of dark corridors to get to the kitchens. It was very old fashioned.

The shul was full of guests and when the bride was late by an hour, I drove to her house. Her father answered the door. I asked him what was going on and he told me she couldn't make her mind up about being married. I told him she had better hurry up and decide as the guests were waiting, and the dinner was cooking. He went and spoke with her and she decided to go ahead. The dinner was controversial because the bar charged for drinks. In those days, at Jewish dos, the bar was usually free, but the father had decided against it. There were many disgruntled people that evening.

At one Prince of Wales Hotel wedding, the dessert was sherry trifle, which we made ourselves. They were all ready except for the cream topping. Twenty trifles in glass dishes, one for each table, were laid out side by side on a trestle waiting for the final decoration. Twenty trifles slid onto the floor as the trestle table collapsed. Luckily they mostly stayed in the dishes. Twenty trifles were put back together and then decorated with cream. There was nothing else to do. The only complaint we got was when a woman sent back the soup for being too hot. We let it sit for ten minutes then sent it out again.

One of the strangest events I catered was an all male charity do for "The Knights of Charity" at the Floral Hall when there were topless waitresses, that I had not hired. The after dinner entertainment was some very raunchy strippers who did interesting things with feather boas. Some of my waitresses refused to work alongside the topless girls and I had to respect that. Later when the show was over and my staff were eating dinner in the kitchens, the guy who was the shammas, whose job it was to make sure that we were being properly kosher in everything we did, came to me to tell me that the artistes had not had anything to eat, and he was willing to take their meals to them in the dressing rooms next to the stage. He was gone a long time.

I was making good money and we decided to build an extension on the back of the house. We went away on holiday after agreeing the plans with a builder. We hired a large motorised caravan and toured around France for two weeks. One of the best days was fishing on a trout farm where we caught our own fish and cooked it that evening. Heidi slept on the top bunk under the roof and we bathed her in the sink.

When we got back the builder had let us down and had done nothing, so we hired another builder we knew called Mr Grimes. We called him "Slimey Grimey". He did a good job though. We had another odd job man who did work for us. He wore a little cowboy hat and always had a roll-up cigarette in his mouth. His name was Mr. Bond, not James, Ken. Whenever he came to size up a job, he would shake his head; take a drag on his cig, and say, "Ropey, very ropey".

In my role of psychotherapist, I have sat with people for thousands of hours as they share their most intimate stories, feelings and thoughts with me. I have been granted access to worlds that would have been closed to me, as we struggled together with the difficulties of being a person in this society at this time. What I have learned is that we are all very, very similar. Sure, we have our individual stories but my thoughts and feelings are not unique to me. There is a commonality of experience in that we blame the past and present circumstances of our lives for how we are. Even as we forgive we are apportioning fault.

Whatever scheme I am involved in, however I am presenting myself, whatever my current act is, I am always me. The I that I refer to when I say, "I thought that, I feel that, I did that, I want that", the me that I refer to when I say, "Give that to me, that is mine" is not who I am, it is who I do. More exactly it is who is being done, who is being felt, who is being thought. Part of my induction into being a fully paid up member of the human being club was to confuse who I am with who is being done.

I have spent a lot of time over the years searching for the answer that would transform my life; some teaching, some person, some vital piece of information. I have amassed a great storehouse of stuff with its own cross reference system but none of this is transformational. It might have altered the way I am with people and myself, it might have even made me a nicer person to be around, but the nature of desire is that there is never enough and there was never enough of the kind of information I desired.

Chapter Thirteen

The Looking Glass Looks Back

It was 1978 that Carole persuaded me to meet Alan Phillips, a jewellery lecturer at Southport College of Art. He was a guitar player and the idea was that we would form a band together. We had a fairly awkward first meeting but decided to go ahead. He was a tall, gangly man and obviously a good guitarist, much better than me, but I have never thought of myself as a musician, more an interpretive singer of songs and a songwriter. I didn't have an electric guitar or an amplifier, so when we actually started practising I used Alan's old guitar and a Selmer valve amp. We decided to form a band, not a punk band as such because we were probably too old but with that punk ethos. Some of the lyrics were sexual, some controversial, some could be seen as misogynistic, but we were sending up the whole PC thing. To this end and after much debate we decided to call ourselves, "The Marital Aids".

After my friend Robert Broudie took me to see the hot Liverpool band, Big in Japan at the Masonic Pub on Berry Street, whose members included his brother Ian Broudie, later of the Lightening Seeds, Holly Johnson, of Frankie Goes to Hollywood fame, Bill Drummond later of KLF and Zoo, Dave Balfe of Zoo, and the outrageous Jane Casey, playing a song called "Big in Japan", as part of their set, I wrote our own anthem "Marital Aids". Here are some of the "offensive" lyrics,

"Rubber wear and frilly knicks
Stiletto heels and rawhide whips
Put other lovers in the shade
Buy yourself a marital aid
In out, in out, in out, in out"

If you come before you've been
Use KY jelly and Vaseline
Put other lovers in the shade
Buy yourself a marital aid
In out, in out, in out, in out"

We recruited other band members, Jonathan Woolston on bass who sported a bandana round his neck, and Duncan Birrell on drums who had a little moustache. Then we decided we needed a girl singer and we asked Maggie Lewis the sixteen year old daughter of the College principal, and then Antoinette Keene, Jonathan's girlfriend, to sing backing vocals.

We set about buying a PA system, microphones etc, and I went back to Frank Hessey's in Liverpool and bought myself a left-handed pre CBS Strat, which I restrung right handed, and a vintage Vox AC30 with blue speakers, the Beatles amp which bands were still using. We practised at the Mount Pleasant pub on Manchester Road and then at Formby Hall in the woods, which was derelict then.

Our first gig was at the Lancaster rooms under the Scarisbrick Hotel on Lord Street in Southport. The scruffy entrance was down the side in Scarisbrick Avenue which led up to the promenade. We went down very well and it became our home gig. We played there several time over the next two years and acquired a following who knew all the songs and sang along. In those days I had a big mop of black hair and a very bushy beard and I wore a long white workman's coat on stage. I always got into a state before we went on and couldn't speak at all. We also played at three "Rock at the Riverside" events, in 1978 and 1979, becoming top of the bill. One of the other bands once wore "We Hate Marital Aids" T shirts.

In December 1978 we played the Arts Ball at the Midnight Lounge. I also fulfilled an ambition and we played at Eric's on Mathew Street in Liverpool, a venue where all the top new bands played. We saw Elvis Costello there at the start of his career and X Ray Spex with the wonderful Poly Styrene.

A few years ago we visited the Tate Gallery in Liverpool and in the music section was a selection of artefacts from Eric's. It was strange to see the membership card that we once had, displayed as history.

After the Eric's gig, Duncan said he was leaving under pressure from his dad who wanted him to study more. He later became a public prosecutor. So we held drumming auditions at Formby Hall and Maurice Cheetham joined us. I knew he was a great drummer as soon as I heard him. He later had a proper career as a percussionist with many famous musicians, singers and orchestras. Jonathan also left us and Geoff, Alan's brother, known as Horace Dogson, who had been doubling on rhythm, took over on bass.

We played at colleges including Manchester Poly and Edge Hill in Ormskirk and Oscar's Club in Hanover Street in Liverpool, The Fleece Hotel in St Helens, the Pear Tree in Bamber Bridge and twice at the Masonic in Berry Street. That was a great gig, a small venue with everybody packed in. On one occasion I was catering a dinner for the Masons in Southport on the same night we had a gig at the Masonic in Liverpool. The dinner finished at nine or so and I drove over to Liverpool still with my tux on and got there just in time to walk on stage. From one world to another connected strangely by Masons.

A guy called Kevin did the special effects which were mostly explosions. At a youth club in Stockport we almost blew up an audience member and set fire to the stage. I still have a £2 receipt for flash powder he bought from the Ace Place in Dale Street, Liverpool.

We hired a guy with a massive PA system for a while which he brought to a gig at the Band on the Wall in Manchester and it picked up noises from the bar every time a pint was pulled. I got really pissed off so after the gig I sacked him. I wore a tux again and Maggie wore a full wedding dress. Carole dressed her in the van outside.

We did an hour long radio interview on the Saturday Rock Show for Manchester Radio interspersed with songs we had recorded with Phil Bush at Arrow Studios and later at Pluto. Phil worked with the Smiths, John Cooper Clarke, the Buzzcocks, Joy Division and many more. Radio Piccadilly recorded four songs with us at Pennine Studios in Oldham with Mark Radcliffe producing. They were featured on the Mike Shaft radio show in Manchester. Several recording companies were interested in our song "Magic Kiss" which we recorded with Phil Bush in 1979 but it never happened.

A strange gig was at the Welcome Inn in Blackpool. We were booked for two nights and we were not what they expected at all, so they cancelled the second night and didn't want to pay us but I wasn't standing for that. We stayed over in a little B&B and it was so cold we slept with our coats on. In the afternoon we were walking through Blackpool and Export were playing at the club/bar "Jenks". Alan Phillips knew them, and we borrowed their equipment and did four songs.

This was the only time that Heidi who was four or five saw the band but she doesn't remember, shame. She was going to school by this time at Larkfield Primary on Preston New Road, just round the corner. She was incredibly social and a natural empath even then, although school was not her thing. One of our favourite little outings was to walk to Botanic Gardens nearby. It had a boating lake with ducks, council style gardens, a fern house, aviary, museum, and tea room. We would view the birds, feed the ducks and walk over the little bridge and around the lake. Once it really poured out of a blue sky and we got so soaked that we didn't care anymore and sang "Singing in the Rain" all the way home, squelching in our shoes. She was a lovely little girl and has grown up into a fine woman with a big heart, always sociable and interested in people. I am immensely proud of her.

I was still working in the shop with my Dad, running my catering firm, and playing in the band, and yet another world opened up for me.

Late in the 70s, Hazel Clyne, after being at the Bristol Old Vic, moved to London to further her acting career. We kept in touch and would occasionally drive down to see her. She lived in a flat at 24a Battersea Rise over a frame shop called Ingo Fink. It was major cool being there as she knew many people in the acting world and would tell the funniest stories.

I have to admit that I have always been strangely susceptible to altered states. I was always being told that I was in a world of my own, although that would not adequately describe where I went, not in my head, but out of my body.

When I was a young teenager one of the games I played with my friends was hypnosis. Charles Hepworth's dad, Sydney, was a doctor and interested in medical hypnosis, and he had long playing records of hypnotic inductions and trance. Several of us, including Carole and Hazel would lie down on the floor, and someone would put a hypnotic record on.

The line that became famous in our group was when we were told that our right hand was getting lighter and lighter and was "Like a balloon." It became a saying in our regular card school with Charles, Nigel Elton, Albert King and others; "My hand is like a balloon.", though I didn't play in it much. Listening to the record, I would be tranced-out almost immediately. They once hypnotised me and told me that I was no longer ticklish and I became able to control my reaction to being tickled. The other weird game we played became known as the "Yenidje Ceremony". It was based on the Balkan Sobranie cigarettes that we pretentiously smoked that contained yenidje tobacco. It involved a pedestal ashtray and a one stringed bow instrument owned by John Taylor and some kind of dance.

Hazel had become interested in est or Erhard Seminar Training. It was initiated in California in the early 1970s by Werner Erhard. In the popular press he is often described as an ex used car salesman and a con artist who made millions out of the new age need of the self obsessed "Me Generation". He had trawled through most of the New Age stuff on offer in California in the late 1960s, including Scientology and Mind Dynamics, eventually forming his own organisation based on "Transformation" and "Getting It". Getting it means that what is... is, and that what isn't... isn't.

If you dip into it a bit it all sounds a bit hippyish and full of circular jargon, but going to the workshops and experiencing them is very different. Well it was for me. Most of the trainings and workshops I have been to in England in my training as a psychotherapist and in CPD events have borrowed elements and language from est without even realising it.

In 1980, Carole and I did not do to the standard training first, but for some reason we did "The Communication Workshop". The format was very similar to the training itself. It was held over two weekends in the ballroom of a large London hotel. There were two hundred participants. It was £200 each.

We stayed with Hazel who had already done the training. Heidi stayed with Mum and Dad but always wanted to come with us on our trips to London, which eventually she did. We went to the hotel and signed in and had to contract not to use any of the material for other purposes. We went into the ballroom where a stage had been set up at one end and rows of chairs were facing it. You could see the workshops as a long shlep, where the trainer shouted a lot and called us all assholes.

What was most interesting was that all breaks were prescribed but not advertised. How much water to drink not knowing when the next toilet break might be or when we were even going to finish for the night brought up all my routines and what I believed I was entitled to.

It's difficult to say what I got from the training but it seemed like a new way of experiencing the world, and of experiencing myself as a person. Did it make my life easier? No. But it gave me a glimpse of how attached I was to my point of view, to my opinions, and that I was little more than a repetition machine using the past as an excuse for my weaknesses and failures. It made me question what I meant by "I" and the amount of significance "I" assigned to itself in the shape of my thoughts and inner experience. I got that the world is meaningless and the possibilities that arise in getting that meaning originates from me, moment by moment.

Another instalment was going to a Douglas Harding workshop at the Friends Meeting House opposite Euston station. It was called the "Headless Way". I recommend his book "On Having No Head", an illuminating and annoying book that challenges who you believe yourself to be. We sat in the balcony and tried the experiments described in that book. It was another brick removed from the mirrored wall of routines in which I had encased myself.

I began to discover books that also opened me to seeing the world in new ways. I read Krishnamurti and obtained an audio tape of one of his talks. Carole and I had a private joke where we would say "Can the Mind?" trying to mimic his strange intonation. Then I was introduced to the Carlos Castaneda books. I read all the ones that had already been published and as the new one came out I would read it in a night. Wonderful stuff.

Then there was the "Tao Teh Ching", the "Diamond Sutra", and books by the crazy guru Rajneesh now known as Osho, and other more complicated classics, like "Zen and the Art of Motorcycle Maintenance". I was devouring information and I realised that people had been struggling with life and death and meaning for centuries, and that even though what they had learned was expressed in different ways, so much of these teachings overlapped.

The next series of events that drastically changed the course of my life was meeting Jenny O'Connor. Hazel introduced her to us. She said that she had been to a workshop given by an English woman who was a psychic channel for an incarnate entity called The Nine. The Nine used the energy of the star Sirius B to communicate through Jenny and you could ask them any question about anything.

Jenny had started as a psychic and was in the papers in 1978 for helping the police with a missing boy. The Nine had not come into the picture yet and whatever was coming thorough her then was called "Whitehead".

And so, after much deliberation, Carole and I decided to book a weekend with Jenny and The Nine. It was in 1980 between us taking the two est workshops. We did the training in 1981.

Again we left Heidi with Mum and Dad and drove down to London and stayed at Hazel's.

Jenny lived at 91 Princethorpe House, a high rise in Paddington, but the workshop was held in an empty Victorian flat somewhere in London with high ceilings and ornate plaster roses around the lights. It was grand, but in need of some decoration. It cost £50 each for two days.

We turned up and we were let in by Judy Marcell who I found out later was from Sacramento and had something to do with est. She was married for a while to Joseph Marcell the actor.

People slowly arrived until there was about twelve of us. We all sat on cushions on the floor. At one end of the room was a mattress. Eventually, about half an hour late, Jenny appeared with her entourage. There was Russell Rae, Alice Anne Parker, Dorette Engi and Trevor Alston. Jenny, Russell, Judy and Dorette sat on the mattress and a chair was found for Alice Anne.

Later I found out who these people were. Russell was a Kiwi and Jenny's boyfriend, he had a broken nose and all the girls fancied him. Dorette was a Swiss girl, an Alexander teacher and worked at the East-West Centre in London. She bankrolled Jenny for a while and had a brief fling with Billy, Jenny's brother. Alice Anne was tall, thin and a bit scary. She was a psychic who has written books about dreams and who now lives in Hawaii. Trevor was the scribe. He wrote down everything that was said in the workshops and turned them into transcripts. He had once worked for Hansard in the Houses of Parliament. The first time we visited Jenny's flat, Trevor answered the door wearing a strap-on pyramid on his head.

Well eventually the day started and I have to say I was not impressed. Jenny didn't actually do any channelling. It was mostly awareness exercises which were ok as far as it went, but not what I had expected which was a bit more cosmic and whizz bang. At the end of the day, she announced we were going to do a meditation. It was getting dark by now and all the long curtains were drawn and we were instructed to lie down.

I couldn't see much so I closed my eyes. I can't remember what she was saying as I was paying most attention to myself, grumbling that the day had been a waste of time and that although there was a carpet on the floor I wasn't even on carpet but on bare floorboards.

Then without warning my chest opened up, and like a fiery comet I flew up and out of my body, up through the Earth's atmosphere and out into space. I circled the earth a few times, and then did a grand tour of the solar system until I reached what seemed like the edge. I looked back and I could see the Earth. It was beautiful, shining, and blue. I headed back home. However being unaccustomed to this mode of travel, I hit my body far too fast. I sat up with what seemed like every atom in my body shaking.

Everyone was looking at me, and Jenny asked us to sit in a circle holding hands and I passed the energy around the circle. Eventually they took me to a local Angus Steak House and bought me a very rare steak which grounded me. It was very dramatic and I got the whizz bang.

The next day was much as the first with the addition of Jenny doing some channelling. This consisted of someone asking a question and Jenny immediately writing on a big yellow lined paper pad without her pen leaving the paper. I later found out it was called automatic writing. She then read out the answer. I saw the writing many times after that and it was quite difficult to read at first but was decipherable.

In the evening we all lay down again and I wondered what was in store for me this time. If my experience the night before had been physical, in that I was still me and experiencing the world through my senses, this time it was entirely different. Something happened but what I am about to describe to you is a poor version of what really happened. Again I went out of my body, not as a comet but somehow out, and this time it was not into the solar system or anything recognisable as this reality at all. At the time it was happening I was not. There was no Geoffrey. There was no centre to experience from or anyone to do the experiencing. I wasn't just headless, I was body-less.

Language is difficult here because it demands a subject, a verb, and an object, but it wasn't like that. It was more like Martin Buber's "I Thou" world, or Krishnamurti's Choiceless Awareness, or in the Tao Teh Ching where Lao Tsu says, "Ever desiring one sees the manifestations, ever desireless one sees the mystery.

I have to say "I", so I was in this field of colour and music, and the music and the colour were one. In all this there were lines, millions of them and in the lines were little shapes like a crooked finger, and they were dancing. Everything was everything else, there was no up or down, no direction at all. I may have been singing, but there was no time, no Geoffrey. I would have stayed there because it was everything and there was nowhere else to go and no one to do any going.

Then there was something interrupting, something that was not everything. It was a noise that seemed to come down a long tunnel. Then I knew what it was, because the noise became a word, my name, Geoffrey. It was Jenny whispering my name into my ear and I was here again. I didn't speak for quite a while. For years I have only shared this with a few people.

These experiences made me want to meet Jenny more and over the next few years we travelled down to London to do more workshops and became a part of the Nine study group. The only person we continued to be friends with outside of the group apart from Hazel was Steve Halliwell who is a wonderful musician and talented keyboard player. He was later in Shriekback and toured America supporting Simple Minds. In the November of 1985, when we lived near Santa Cruz, we saw them play at the Kaiser Convention Centre in Oakland. We went backstage and got a rarefied whiff of how huge bands like Simple Minds were treated. Steve was later in King Swamp and now plays in LiTTLE MACHiNe.

The workshops were not always sweetness and light. During an early one in Jenny's high rise flat there was about twenty of us sitting in a circle. There was a break and everyone was chatting. Jenny was opposite me. We looked at each other. She leaned forward and in a quiet voice she said,

"If Carole had the chance to further her career as an artist and it meant leaving you, would you let her go?"

I was taken aback with the question but without hesitation I replied,

"Of course"

It was the right answer. It was the expected answer. She smiled and said,

"You're a fucking liar."

The force of her words threw me back. Then the break was over and the workshop continued. I didn't speak for the rest of the evening. The awful thing for me was she was right. This exchange was the first of many "in my face" challenges over the next few years.

The study group would meet regularly when Jenny was in England. The rest of the time she was at Esalen Institute, in Big Sur, California. Esalen was on Highway One, south of Monterey, on the cliffs between the Pacific and the Lucia Mountains. It was originally a hot springs resort but, taken on by Dick Price and Michael Murphy, it became the leading centre in America for New Age and alternative ways of being.

Many well known New Age and psychology heavyweights such as B.F. Skinner, Carl Rogers, RD Laing, Gregory Bateson, Werner Erhard, Paul Tillich, Aldous and Laura Huxley, Alan Watts, Charles Tart, Ida Rolf and Abraham Maslow took part in events there. John Lilly, whose life was later shown in the film "Altered States", began his experiments with flotation tanks and ketamine there. Fritz Perls became a workshop leader in 1963 and Will Schutz who wrote the bestseller "Joy" was brought in.

In 1969, Joan Baez organised a Folk Music Festival around the outdoor pool on the cliffs overlooking the Pacific. The line up included, Crosby, Stills, Nash and Young, Joni Mitchell, and John Sebastian. Esalen history is well documented and has many conspiracy theories connected to the workshop leaders and New Age spirituality and its political influences, especially the Nine. Anyway, Jenny and Russell travelled back and forth between London and Esalen where she and the Nine were workshop leaders and the Nine were in the Esalen Catalogue.

We were still involved with est and when we heard that a communication workshop was to be held in Leeds we volunteered to assist. Being an assistant meant attending the workshop but also setting it up and taking it down. There were very strict rules as to how things must be done.

I remember going to see Werner speak at Wembley in 1979 or 80. The theatre was totally cleaned by the assistants. Everything had to be done with integrity. It was just him on stage with some flowers on a table next to him. I enjoyed it as much as the training. I loved to listen to him speak and I still do. There are many video and audio recordings of Werner on YouTube. I recommend "The Heart of the Matter". A film was recently made about him called "Transformation" by Robyn Symon.

The Leeds workshop was led by a trainer called Stephen. A few months later one of the tabloids did an est expose and ran pictures of Stephen dubbing him the most evil man in Britain.

They said all the participants were being brainwashed and exploited. My brain certainly needed a good wash.

Roger Potter, Hazel's husband at the time, came to Leeds to assist with us. One of the tasks I was assigned to do was with Roger. On the Sunday morning, the second day, we were told to get two large portable blackboards. We were in a strange town, where we didn't know anyone, and it was Sunday, but we just had to do it, no questions asked, and we did. We looked in the phone directory and after a few hours found a school janitor who knew where there were two spare backboards.

We triumphantly took them back to the workshop room where they were never used, but we had used our intention and made it happen, that was the point.

A harder lesson was at the very end of the workshop on the Sunday evening. The rule was that for the entire workshop an assistant would be stationed outside the door almost like the Tyler of a Masonic lodge. I was picked and for the last hour of the day I was on the "wrong" side of the door. On the "right" side I could hear people whooping and celebrating and partying.

My mind was supplying all the pictures to go along with that, together with a nonstop diatribe of how unfair it was that I was there and how could they treat me like this, I, who had put so much work into setting it up and making sure it ran smoothly, I, who had acted unselfishly and out of the goodness of my heart. My self-importance reached critical levels that evening.

By then I was no longer in the catering business and I had stopped working with Dad. I had just had enough of being a butcher. I had been in the shop for nearly seventeen years. It was a difficult decision because I felt I was letting Dad down, but I also felt I was letting myself down and I wanted to do something different with my life. I cried when I told my parents I was leaving the shop. I sold all the catering equipment by auction through Tony Webber in Ormskirk. It was strange to watch the plates, the ovens, the cutlery etc go under the hammer bit by bit, but I needed to do it.

One of the events that informed my decision was the Southport Kashrus Commission giving Norman Forshaw, an ex-employee, a licence to sell kosher poultry. He had learned the trade in our shop and it felt like another betrayal. Over the years we had a procession of non-Jewish butchers working for my Dad. There was George Whipp, Cliff Meadows, and one of the most memorable, a man we always called "Joe 90" because he looked so like Gerry Anderson's character.

We had an assistant who I caught stealing from us. One day I went out to the alley at the back of the shop to put something in the dustbin. They had just been emptied but one was half full. I pulled out what was there and someone had jammed a piece of a cardboard box halfway down and underneath were steaks and chickens and chops all neatly wrapped up. Dad called the police and that evening they waited out of sight to see who would turn up. It was Harry, they arrested him and Dad sacked him. We were later told that he had been selling around the local pubs for some time.

So the shul decided that we should not have a monopoly in Southport and the Commission contacted Norman and offered him a licence, which he accepted. He opened a shop in Ashley Road around the corner from the shul. The Jewish population in Southport was declining as people died or moved away and our income was declining with it, although it was a common belief that we were making a fortune. The shul's attitude was always the same.

In 1975 they had discussed our turnover and made the decision to increase the annual tax we paid them, called shechita money, to £1,000 a year. They never had the foresight to realise that by making it unprofitable for us to continue and eventually close, they would lose the tax that they did little for as well as losing one of the integral bricks that kept the community viable.

When Dad retired in 1982, he attempted to sell the shop as a going concern but no-one was interested. He had to sell the equipment off to butchers around town. Sadly, the Southport Jewish community continued its decline and these days shul attendance is so low that the basement of the shul, the Bais Hamedrish, is often used for services.

We sold our home in Mallee Crescent and moved to 15 Cock Robin Cottages in Croston between Preston and Chorley. The terraced cottages were all in a row off Highfield Road and up a track. They were originally built for the estate workers. We had a huge goodbye party in our old house with a bonfire and a barbecue.

Our cottage was at the far end and you had to walk between the cottages and their front gardens to get there. It was next to a grassy field the same height as the eaves on the roof where horses were kept. The front door was French windows into the lounge and then a large kitchen. An open staircase led upstairs to the bedrooms and bathroom. The walls were thick and the window-sills deep. There was a paved back yard with an outside toilet and in the summer it was heaven to sit there with the door open and look across the fields. We would often go for a walk along the banks and over the bridge of the River Yarrow that ran through the village.

We hired the builder and handyman Mr. Bond to dismantle and re-erect the wooden ice cream shed we bought that had stood over the old bridge across the Marine Drive in Southport. It had a pull down flap for serving customers. We had walked past it one day and seen it was for sale as the owner was retiring. Mr. Bond had put it in the back garden at Mallee Crescent for us, and we didn't want to lose it, so we asked him to move it again to the front garden at Cock Robin. It was Carole's ceramic studio, although at Croston we put our washing machine in it as well.

I was signing on for a while and in those days they also paid your mortgage, but then I got a job working for All White Taxis on Eastbank Street in Southport. I picked the coldest winter for years to be a taxi driver. I knew Southport well from my delivery boy days in the shop, so even though it was before Satnavs, that wasn't a problem. It was so cold that the edge of the sea froze, like a weird sloppy jelly. The roads were thick with hardened bumps of snow. I would go to Mum and Dad's in Saunders Street every few hours to warm up.

I didn't last long as a taxi driver. The more experienced drivers had the jump on me responding to a call from the controller quicker than I did, often telling a lie about where they were located in order to get the job. I was advised to carry a baseball bat under my seat in case of trouble and, although I didn't, hearing that really put me off the job.

By now Marital Aids had disbanded and I was in a new band with Maurice Cheetham on drums, Phil Johnson, who later became a headmaster, on sax and keyboards, and Steve Mantle on fretless bass. We never played any live gigs but in 1980 we recorded four tracks with Phil Bush at Pluto in Granby Row, Manchester. It was owned by two of Herman's Hermits. We were called "Luminous Beings" after my love of the Carlos Castaneda books. We were described as an avant-garde jazz punk band.

Three of these tracks were featured on a vinyl album compilation released by Skeleton records in Birkenhead, Liverpool, called " ....a trip to the dentist". It's a collector's item these days. Then I wrote songs for a band sometimes called "Madama" sometimes "Masque of Bizarro". We recorded "Android Love" "Girl of the Golden West", "Real Modern Girl" and "I Almost Lost My Mind". Maria Cavanagh, of short blond hair and great voice, was the lead singer.

We went to London to see Jenny regularly and one occasion took Heidi with us to a wedding of two people in the Nine group. By then, on one of our trips, we had bought a green, soft, toy turtle for her she called "Turty", which Heidi still treasures. The wedding was held in the back garden of someone's house on a lovely sunny day. Heidi and Jenny met and immediately made a deep connection. They spent a long time together sitting together at the back door of the house. They decided they were in the same dream. We began exchanging letters through 1981 and 1982.

That summer the Falklands war ended and there was a victory parade through Croston. Most of the village turned out and there was a brass band and bunting. Everyone seemed very happy. I was not happy. I found it hard to believe that people could celebrate killing others as a victory like that. Jenny had been encouraging us to go to California, and we decided to take the plunge into deep water and go. We put our house on the market. Our solicitor, Noel Adler, advised us against it, but we were determined.

I decided that never having been away from home for an extended period of time it would be a good idea to have a sort of dry run closer to home, although it didn't turn out like I intended. Hazel knew someone we could stay with for a while in Rotterdam so I bought a backpack for each of us and booked a plane to Amsterdam without pre-booking a hotel. When we arrived we found a small hotel easily enough and phoned the person in Rotterdam. He said it was fine to come and we could stay as long as we liked. We took the train to Rotterdam and found where he lived.

He welcomed us in and made us tea. It was a big old house in the downtown area and it turned out he was a cannabis dealer. He lived in a large front room stuffed with old furniture, with a massive leather armchair where he sat. There was a pair of scales on the table and ready made up bags. People were constantly knocking at the door to buy off him and some of them looked and sounded very unsavoury.

He told us he sold the best dope in Rotterdam and that we could help ourselves to as much as we wanted. His wife was away for a few days, but he was expecting her back the following evening. She was a professional roller skater.

The next day we walked around the area for a while and then returned. There was an altercation with a customer and he pulled a gun and got the man to leave. I thought we really have to get out of here but it was late in the evening and so I decided to stay the night and leave first thing in the morning. We were sleeping in the kitchen on camp beds with a mosquito candle burning. His wife arrived home late and we could hear them having noisy sex for what seemed like hours. Their bed was banging against the adjoining wall. In the morning, he seemed surprised when we said we were leaving and I have to say he had been most hospitable. We went back to Amsterdam and returned to England after a few days.

Hazel, Carole, and I had been leading awareness workshops we called "Playshops" at the East West Centre in London, and Bob Leach had been one of the participants. We did exercises to bypass the logical mind like, "I am a Laughing Ho Ho." I demonstrated it first then everyone had a go. It was sung to the tune of "I am a Laughing Policeman" and was accompanied by shaking the belly as you laughed. The idea was to actually become a "Laughing Ho Ho". Each person stood up and sang it to the group. You could try it for yourself. We also did a workshop for all the people who shared a large house with Bob. It was filmed by Martin Sixsmith who years later became famous as the writer of "The Lost Child of Philomena Lee", which became the film, "Philomena".

We knew that when we were in California, we couldn't stay at Esalen or with Jenny, so we contacted Bob, who had emigrated there and now lived in Benicia, near San Francisco, and he agreed to let us stay with him

We sold Cock Robin and I cried as we drove away for the last time. I loved that house. We went to stay with Manny, Carole's Dad, on Lulworth Road in Southport for a few weeks until our flight to San Francisco. It was September 1982 and getting cold. The flat had lovely gardens at the front but inside was musty and in need of decoration. He was not doing well financially and he would use the stove as heat sometimes.

We left a big trunk of stuff in the cellar at Saunders Street; gave our bed to the girl in the end cottage at Cock Robin; moved our two large drapers drawers and our plaster bird collection to our friend Vince Kelly in Skelmersdale; our antique desk that we had bought when we were in the flat in Bold Street to Mum; and my record player and records and our Renault car to Maurice

Cheetham. I have to say the car was not in the best of condition. We gave other furniture like a marble top washstand to whom? I don't know. We forgot.

Paul drove us the Manchester where we got the coach to Heathrow and off we went on our mad adventure wondering what the consequences of our decision might be.

I have involved myself in some kind of spiritual search since the late 1970s. I wanted to live a different kind of life, not just the life that had been prescribed for me. I wanted to be a better person, and although I justified my search by telling myself my goal was to be more compassionate and empathic, by better I really meant smarter and more powerful. It was another strategy for me to try to boost my self-importance and vanity. I was still being a greedy consumer. I had just shifted the focus of my appetite.

Maybe that was necessary. Maybe I had to gorge myself on new spiritual insights and information until I threw up. In therapy, if the relationship lasts long enough, the client arrives at an "Oh my God" moment when the person realises their part in what has happened in their lives. It's all very well talking about the theory of taking responsibility for your experience, but when it comes to actually coming from that, the shock can be enormous because it really means taking responsibility for all of it, not just the nice stuff. This is where you need to get off your high horse and laugh at yourself or you get trapped in a huge and heavy self importance.

Chapter Fourteen

The Revolving Door of Choice

After a long flight, Bob Leach was waiting for us at the airport in San Francisco. He had rented a car from "Rent-A-Wreck" in Walnut Creek, a town close to where he lived in Benicia. They rented big second-hand American cars. We drove onto the highway and stopped off at a "Denny's" diner for a drink and something to eat. They put a red and yellow plastic Denny's timer on the table and if your order was not delivered within a certain time, it was free. We had a coffee and the waitress gave us iced water as well. It was dark out and with all the lights and the neon shining, it was like being in a film of California that I had seen so often on the screen but now we were in it.

It was late when we arrived, and we met Sandy, Bob's girlfriend, and his mother who was not so friendly. Sandy's son was asleep in bed. If you know the Halloween street scene in the movie "E.T.", then you will know what Bob's house and street looked like. Actually we went to see the movie soon after we got there. We went to bed exhausted.

In the morning we awoke and had breakfast with Bob. Then we got changed into swimming costumes, we soon learned to say swimsuits, and went out into the back garden. Sandy thought we were crazy sunbathing in September, but to us it was in the twenties centigrade. It got hotter over the next few weeks and as we did not have a car we did a lot of walking in the hot sun. We had our own bedroom with a large walk-in closet which we made into a tiny bedroom for Heidi. In the afternoon I drove the hire car over to Walnut Creek and Bob followed on his motor bike. We drove home with me on the back.

One of the reasons we had gone to California was in the hope that we might meet one of Carole's ceramic heroes, Bob Arneson. One day we walked into Benicia town centre which was just one long dusty street with wooden sidewalks. Carole wanted to buy some art supplies, so we went to the only art shop in town. Carole noticed a small Arneson print in the window. She asked the owner why she had the piece there and the woman told her that Bob Arneson's studio was right across the street. What wonderful serendipity.

At first Carole was a bit nervous about just knocking on his door, but Bob went over and arranged for them to meet. I went with Carole and Arneson was immediately friendly, smiling, and welcoming. He, like his work, exuded presence. The studio was huge, light and airy with a balcony and it opened out into a lovely garden. Bob's work was on the right and his wife's work, Sandra Shannonhouse, was on the left.

He and Carole got on straight away and he got her to help him in whacking a leather-hard sculpture with big sticks. It was one of his "War Series", a generic, giant head on a pedestal. He was into what he called the "Force of Nature" being present in his work which could mean what happened in the making or in the kiln. Bob's assistant, George, was also there. Although Carole knew his work, he was not particularly well known by the public until the summer of 1981, only a year or so before we arrived. He had been commissioned to make a bust of George Moscone for the city of San Francisco for the newly opened Moscone Centre. Moscone had been murdered along with the gay activist Harvey Milk, by Dan White. A film was made about it starring Sean Penn.

When the sculpture was presented to Mayor Dianne Feinstein, it was decided that it was too controversial and it was rejected and given back to Arneson. It was this publicity that got him in the public eye. The city of San Francisco has only recently bought it back. He was still adjusting to his notoriety when we met him.

Arneson was Professor of Ceramics at the University of California at Davis in the famous TB9 studio, and he offered Carole her own studio there with use of clay and equipment in exchange for her doing some teaching, starting in the spring of 1983. We said yes, although we had no idea where Davis was. We found that it was near Sacramento and contacted a realtor there called Lou Bellou, and we arranged to rent an apartment at 1205 5th Street in Davis.

In the meantime, Bob Leach who was into est and was in charge of audio recording for them, found out that Werner, after a long gap, was going to be the trainer at a training in October 1982. He asked if we would like to go. As graduates of the training we were entitled to attend other trainings for free, but only as observers. We put our names down and got tickets. The event was at est headquarters in San Francisco. Carole and I took Heidi with us as she was determined to meet him.

We got there late in the evening and we waited in the reception area for Werner to arrive. We waited quite a while and then Werner swept in with an entourage. Heidi ran over and gave him the bouquet of flowers she had been holding and he stopped, picked her up and hugged her.

We waited until two in the morning to get into the training which went on all night. Heidi was looked after by Bev Kaye who was an est area manager. When the evening was over she invited us to have Thanksgiving dinner with her and her husband Michael. They lived in Redwood City.

Before we went there we decided to go on a little road trip. We took the Greyhound bus to Yosemite National Park and rented a log cabin for a few days. The park is truly beautiful and El Capitan, at over two thousand metres, is awesome. There are posters warning about bears and where to keep food away from them, but one evening we had just left the cabin to go and get some dinner and we heard a loud growl behind us. We turned around and there was a real live bear. It was far enough away so we could run but too close for comfort!

We met a couple who lived in Los Angeles and they invited us to stay with them. They we leaving the next day and we had a few days left so it wasn't until the following week that we took the bus to L.A. By now Heidi had not been at school for several months so I began home tutoring her, and I remember us practising times tables as we travelled on the buses.

It was not a good beginning to our stay in L.A. The bus station is in a dodgy area of town and when we disembarked a big, scary-looking guy spat at Carole. We quickly got a taxi to the address they had given us. When we arrived we discovered the guy had a penchant for hanging upside down from a contraption set up in one of his doorways. He said it was good for his back.

We visited the tar pits, the beach and the Museum of Modern Art. Then we headed north with a stop-over in Bakersfield, a hot dusty place not to be visited again. We stayed with Bob until a few days before Thanksgiving which was November 25th 1982 and we caught the bus to Redwood City, which is about 25 miles south of San Francisco by Highway 101.

Bev and Michael were incredibly hospitable and we enjoyed our first Thanksgiving with them and the giving of thanks and recognising our blessings. Bev had fallen in love with Heidi and they insisted on our staying longer. Bev took Heidi to J.C. Penney and said she could pick any toy. Heidi wanted a big Snoopy but only asked for a small one. She also gave her some of her own teddies.

By now I had finally made contact with Jenny and Russell. They were staying with a friend near a little town called Corralitos in the Watsonville area. They said to come over and stay so we asked Bev and Michael if they would drive us there and they agreed, although we could have probably stayed with them until Christmas at least.

Well the day came and the arrangement was that we would meet Russell in the car park of Albertson's supermarket in Watsonville. It was about a one and a half hour journey south on Highway 280, through Palo Alto, Los Gatos and Santa Cruz. Russell was there waiting for us and we all got out and had a group hug. He asked us to follow him. He was in the big blue car they called "Dozy" because of the registration number that began DZY. We drove into the forest along Browns Valley Road and onto Redwood Road which was the address but the location of the property we were going to was not on the road.

Eventually we turned off onto a dirt and gravel track and stopped at an electronic barrier. Russell punched the code numbers in and we set off and up on a windy track that only just accommodated one vehicle. Up and up we went, deeper into the magnificent redwood forest.

Then we reached the top which was a large flat area where the trees had been cleared. We passed a beautiful round wooden house on the left with a stoop and further on came to the main house. It was a one story building made from the redwoods of the mountain. To the right was a paddock and on the horizon over the rolling redwood mountains was the blue of the Pacific Ocean. There were round tables with umbrellas advertising Cinzano bordered by a garden but the grassy areas were brown and burned from the sun. At the back was an old trailer in a field and a giant fire pit. Opposite the front door stood a large covered log store and a brick fireplace and up a little flowered path was a wooden outdoor shower. Jenny was sitting in an easy chair at the front. Her hair was long and she wore a hippy style long dress. She got up and hugged us and said it was about time we arrived. Bev and Michael did not stay which I later regretted. I think they had not expected to take us to the top of a redwood mountain.

Jenny introduced us to Kai, the woman who owned the property. Her full name was Arcadia Mel de Fontenay Bandini. She had French ancestry. She was slight with a shock of white hair, and piercing blue eyes, maybe in her fifties. She took us inside the first room which was a large kitchen with a central wooden table. The ceiling was glass and sloping with round wooden redwood beams. There was a large lounge to the right with a window seat at the end covered in a floral fabric.

We had tea and sat and chatted. She slept in another of the buildings. She took her dogs out for a long walk every day and then had a nap in the afternoon. That night Heidi slept on the window seat and we all played Rummikub for hours, the first of many such tournament nights. I remember Kai telling Jenny off for being too hard on me as I was just a beginner. This, of course, made no difference as verbal abuse was part of the game.

I found out that Karen and Nina lived in the round house that I'd seen on the way up. Karen was an amazing carpenter and had built the house herself. She was tall and skinny with craggy features and had moved there from Germany. Nina was a teacher; she was round, jolly and very pretty. There was another house some distance away called the Cherry Tree House because a cherry tree grew inside the house and up through the roof. Paulette lived there.

We met Teddy Lyon at Kai's, and we once went to a party at her house nearby and met Erin, her daughter. Teddy was tall, with short gray hair. There was a depth to her that I could feel. She had been the assistant, lover, confidante and secretary of Fritz Perls, the Gestaltist for a great many years. She met him in 1965 and knew him for the rest of his life. It took a special person to put up with him for that long.

She also grew the best outdoor marijuana and once it was my turn to test the new crop. Everybody sat around and a joint was rolled and handed to me. I was supposed to report on my experience but I totally failed. After only two tokes I was unable to speak for several hours.

Kai had met Jenny at Esalen and had many Nine sessions. She was a photographer and film maker. On her desk was one of the very first Apple computers which at that time I didn't understand at all. She was friends with Gregory Bateson and his wife Lois. Bateson was famous for his "Double Bind Theory" and his theories about patterns. Kai was making a film about him but I don't think she ever finished it.

Jenny was coming to the end of her major influence at Esalen at this time. By now I had pieced together some of Jenny and the Nine's history. In 1978 she met Sir John Whitmore, husband of Diana Whitmore. Diana was part of setting up and running the Psychosynthesis Trust in London. John was an ex racing driver and much later became one of the leading figures in the coaching industry. His book "Coaching for Performance" was a best seller. Unfortunately he recently died. John had been in contact with Andrija Puharich, a long time promoter of the Nine. He had associations with Uri Geller, Dr. Vinod, Phyllis Schlemmer, another channel, and Gene Rodenberry of Star Trek fame. John took Jenny to California and introduced her to Betty Fuller at her home in Tiburon near San Francisco.

Betty was a Trager practitioner and a student of Moshe Feldenkrais. She also knew Werner Erhard and was a trainer of est graduates. Werner wanted her to be a full trainer but said that she needed to lose weight first and she refused. Betty also introduced Jenny to Raz Ingrasci an early associate of Werner Erhard and the founder of the "Hoffman Method". Betty was so impressed with Jenny that she took her to Esalen to meet with Dick Price and he invited her to stay. Thus began Jenny and the Nine's ascendancy into being the must meet workshop leaders at Esalen of the time.

All the sessions were recorded and turned into transcripts by Trevor. Many of the leading lights of the New Age had private sessions with her. The Nine were even given reign to change the corporate structure of Esalen after many heated meetings with Dick, Janet Lederman and Julian Silverman. Jenny also had allies in staff like Bette Dingman and workshop leader Janet Zuckerman, known as J.Z.

We stayed with Kai on the mountain for a few days, and made plans to meet up again but it was time to go, so we caught the bus back up north to Bob's.

In the spring of 1983, we moved to Davis near Sacramento. Our apartment was in a semi-circular one story block with a kidney shaped swimming pool in the centre. We had two cups, a frying pan and three blue sleeping bags. It was a nice apartment with a living room and kitchen downstairs and two bedrooms upstairs. There was a washing machine and dryer block by the side of the pool. Most of the residents were students.

Lou Bellou, the realtor, came to welcome us. He wore a short sleeve shirt with a pen in the pocket, a bow tie and slacks. He had a little moustache. Like many people he loved our English accents.

We enrolled Heidi at Valley Oak School. Their only consideration in taking Heidi was which shots she had been given.

We were a few short, so we went to Davis Free Clinic and saw a very friendly doctor called Mark Murray. Heidi's best friends at school were Letty and Melanie, both from poor backgrounds.

We went over to the campus to view Carole's studio. It was about a twenty minute walk. TB9, temporary building number nine, was a long shed with a tin roof. It is still there. It housed a number of studios along a corridor which opened out into a main studio. Bob's studio was first on the left, Carole's last on the right. The kilns were really huge with rollers to roll in large work which most people made. There was a massive old baker's mixing machine where dry clay and water were mixed. Around the outside was an impromptu sculpture garden where old pieces of work were dotted about. When it rained in the winter the noise of the rain on the roof was deafening, and in the summer it was like an oven in there. Talented ceramicists worked there such as Tony Natsoulas and Joe Mannino who was in charge in Bob's absence. Lisa Reinerston had the first studio on the right. I remember her working for ages on a sculpture of a monkey. She had a little daughter called Jessica, who must be in her late forties now.

David Anderson, who became a dear friend, was an undergraduate as was Jim Thornton. Unfortunately, David died this year after a long battle with cancer.

So we got into a new routine, and gradually we bought house stuff from thrift stores like pots and pans and sheets and pillows. Heidi went to school every day and Carole went to TB9 every day. I sat by the pool and did a lot of reading, or sat in Carole's studio and did a lot of reading. Every morning that summer, Heidi would get up early and walk in her pyjamas to the corner of 5th and L, about 3 minutes, and hang out with the people in Domino's Pizza and 7-11.

We even had a little earthquake. One day we were sitting by the pool and all the water in it lifted up and fell out. It wasn't until later that we heard there had been a small earthquake quite a few miles away.

I also learned my lesson, at least for a while, about getting too stoned. A friend of ours had bought us two or three ounces of sensemilla, the seedless buds of the female marijuana plant. We had several buds which we kept in a large jar. They smelled wonderful and were sticky and sparkly. Well, Carole and Heidi went out somewhere and I rolled myself a joint, not meaning to smoke it all. In California we had learned to roll joints without adding tobacco as is the practice in England. I was engrossed in the book I was reading and after a while I looked at the joint and realised I had smoked most of it. I was so stoned I couldn't feel my body.

Carole and Heidi arrived home and I was able to tell them what I'd done. They helped me into the shower where I stayed for about an hour. The water helped to solidify me. As you can imagine it doesn't take much for me to exteriorise.

We all visited with Jenny and Russell again. They were now living in Seaside in Monterey County. We took Highway 680 then 101 past San Jose. It took about three hours. We were given a lift by a young student with a shock of ginger hair called Len Levene. He was a guitar player and vey kindly loaned me a guitar for a while as he knew I was missing playing. Eventually he gave the guitar to me. He was quite freaked out meeting Jenny and hardly spoke for the three days we were there. They were renting a low rise apartment. Janet Zuckerman visited with her husband the Reverend Fred Boeve. She was round and fat, he was tall and thin.

Janet known as J.Z. was a gestalt teacher at Esalen and a big buddy of Jenny who referred to her as "Momma". Her main workshop was called "The Feeling Process." She was a large woman and really into her food. Carole took a workshop with her a year or two later. We just loved hanging out with her. She was funny, loving and very direct. Janet had gone to Esalen originally to take a workshop with Betty Fuller and just stayed. In those days the right people could do that at Esalen.

One workshop exercise was called "Pink Oysters". It was an all woman group and the woman would show their vaginas to each other and be proud of them.

Janet was not an intellectual and her workshops were pure experience. On the first evening of the one Carole did all the participants in the mixed group undressed, were given a lit candle to hold and, with a partner, walked hand in hand down the path to the hot-tubs on the cliffs. Everyone got in and instead of chanting Om, they chanted Yum.

The tubs at Esalen were wonderful. The hot sulphur water came right out of the rock and was held in by big black bungs. If you wanted more hot water you took the bung out. I can be there now, in the evening, in the hot water, steam rising, joss sticks burning, looking out from the cliffs over the pacific under a starry sky.

I think this may be where we first met Darrel MCDowall. Darrel was a tall Aussie very into the spiritual journey. He had been to Poona where the original Rajneesh ashram was and been initiated as a sanyassin although I never saw him in his red robes. He had also been in the army and fought in Vietnam. He often argued with Jenny as he felt that none of us was being practical enough. Over time we became friends.

In 1981, the ashram in Poona had been disbanded and Rajneesh moved to Oregon. Many of his sanyassins went back to their home countries and opened up centres where they taught meditation and studied his teachings. Rajneesh encouraged his disciples to be open about sex and relationships and Darrel was certainly like that. Although later Rajneesh became concerned about the spread of HIV and ordered them to not just wear condoms but also rubber gloves during sex.

Some of the groups in Poona could get quite violent taking the encounter group to its ultimate. Sometime people fought and bones were broken. I was told that little plots of land were bought and sold and the price depended on how close the plot was to Rajneesh when he gave his daily talks. Some sanyassins were in the est training we did and the trainer gave them a hard time about them wearing a picture of Rajneesh in a beaded necklace called a "Mala". They were somewhat defensive about it.

Dick Price went to Poona in 1977, along with J.Z. and other Esalen leaders after reading some of his books and hearing audio tapes. Janet told me that when she was presented to Rajneesh to receive her new name from him, they just sang "Yes" to each other. However, when Dick saw what was going on in the groups he was appalled at their naiveté and the mistakes that were being made and they all left. However, with all that, I personally got a lot out of reading his books which were basically transcriptions of his talks such as commentaries on Jesus or Zen. I was introduced to the mystic Kabir in this way.

In Davis, in the spring of 1983, we moved to an apartment across the pool, and John and Cheryl moved into our old place. She would often swim naked in the pool at night. John was an archetypal California dude. He was tall and thin with long blond hair and a droopy moustache. He was always stoned and a "Deadhead", a follower of the band "The Grateful Dead". They had a TV which we would sometimes watch.

We had an interesting visitor called Dennis, one of Bob Leach's acquaintances. He was a very strange boy, probably in his late twenties. He lived in his very old beaten up car. The driver's seat was worn to the springs. We took him in and he lived with us for a while. He had great difficulty operating in the world, and sometimes he thought he was Jesus. He was sweet though and showed me how to make burritos.

I remember standing with him in the kitchen and chopping up cilantro, what we call coriander, for the sauce mix. One day he called me at Carole's studio asking for help. He said he wanted to walk out and meet us but he was trapped in the apartment. I asked him by what and he told me there were three young females in little bikinis sunbathing by the pool and he dare not walk past them. I did not argue with him as it would have come under the heading of trying to challenge the illogical with logic so I walked back home and rescued him.

A student at TB9 called Diana Browning, who lived in Carmichael, asked us if we would house-sit while she and her husband had a vacation in Hawaii. They had a great house with a pool out back and we said yes. They said I could use their truck but I had to pass my U.S. driving test. I thought, no problem, and took the written test, easy peasey, I had been driving for eighteen years. Then I took the actual driving test and after five minutes the examiner said, "Failed" and asked me to return to the driving centre. I had turned left, like a right in England, illegally. I didn't tell Diana and took my test again and passed in the June.

We told Jenny and Russell and they came to stay for the two weeks and Darrel turned up as well. They started teaching us backgammon and we had all night tournaments like we did with Rummikub. We still play it now. We had a great time swimming, until the pool turned green. It was so hot the chemicals had stopped working. Then one of the water beds got punctured, the dishwasher broke and the drains got blocked. However, Diana was ok about it when they returned and said it often happened. I didn't tell them about our house guests.

Then Bob Leach contacted us to say that he had split with Sandy and could he stay, so Dennis moved on and Bob came to live under our stairs. He wanted a new job and I remember Carole making sure he was dressed properly for his job interview, which he got. He was the only one with a job and would go off to work every day, and in the meantime we were running out of money. We had to do something.

So, Carole got a part time job with Jim Howard and Betty Nelson. They lived on J Street. She had very short red hair and he was a very tall, thin man with a long scraggly hair and beard. They modelled Star War characters, but they hired Carole to model prototypes for other toy figures namely professional wrestlers. The one I remember best is the maquette she made for the wrestler, "Big John Stud". I loved his little bootlaces.

Steve LaVine also worked there and we became friends with Steve and his girlfriend Shannon Sutherland who was a nurse at the time. Steve was also a musician and played the banjo. They lived on Yale Drive and we would hang out there a lot and smoke grass.

Shannon had a friend who was into NLP, which was being developed at the time in Santa Cruz by Bandler and Grinder based on the work of Gregory Bateson, Virginia Satir, Milton H Erickson the hypnotherapist, and to a degree the gestaltist Fritz Perls. He had left some NLP books at her house and I avidly read "The Structure of Magic" and "Frogs into Princes". Popularised NLP has been perverted into a technique driven model these days. Anyway, Big John's bootlaces were a good source of income for us.

Carole and Shannon went into business together making ladies shorts screen-printed with one of Carole's computer cat designs. They hired a small room at the back of an upmarket thrift store and turned it into a printing studio. They sold to the local fashion shops.

At the same time, we found out about a summer camp run by Jane Fonda, on her ranch, and we applied for a scholarship for Heidi to go for two weeks. We were successful and Carole and I, being chronically short of cash by now, decided to take some of the designer label clothes from the thrift store for Heidi to take with her. We took the best stuff so she wouldn't be shown up.

We drove her to Sacramento airport and watched her plane take off to Santa Barbara. She went horse riding and night walking and made art. Heids remembers sitting on Jane's knee and Jane comforting her when she was missing us. I think she had a great time but we missed her terribly too, and we were glad when she returned home safely.

Carole was making large sculptures at TB9. She made a lovely larger than life piece of us hugging, and I remember how long it took us to get it in the kiln. Then she made a ceramic picket fence that stretched the length of her studio with ceramic clouds hanging from the ceiling. We became friends with Bob Arneson and he sometimes invited us to Benicia to have dinner with them.

Through the Uni we met Krysia Lamore and her then boyfriend, Jason. He was young, blond, very tall, and a skateboarder. Krysia was an artist and a beautiful real California hippy. She loved dogs and the one she had then was named, "Blue". We spent many happy times hanging out at her house. I remember a dinner party she hosted where we met Enrique Mendoza, who was a gay Chicano boy and a black couple called Harold and Jolene who moved to San Francisco. We are still friends with Krysia and keep in contact on FB. I heard Talking Heads properly for the first time at her house, especially "Psycho Killer".

By now money was really tight and I saw an advert in the local paper, the "Enterprise", for a window cleaner. I met with Donna Miller, the owner of "Miller Maintenance", and she gave me the job. Her firm employed several people and her main source of work was the contract she had with the students' halls of residence. The students would trash their apartments and in the vacations we would go in and clean from top to bottom. This meant the furniture and carpets, the kitchen, including the oven and fridge, and the windows. The walls were also painted.

The rest of the year it was general weekly house cleaning, and carpet and window cleaning. Donna and I got on well and we soon became friends. She was a bit older than me with short greying hair. She had a daughter and two sons, Cody and Timmy, and Heidi really liked Cody.

Carole also worked with me and I remember one house we cleaned together that had two orange trees in the front garden. It was a fortnightly clean and no matter how well we cleaned it the next time we went it was filthy again. I especially remember the glass doors at the back which were covered in mud from the dogs jumping up. We had to scrape the dirt off with razor blades. I enjoyed the carpet cleaning best. Donna had a large blue industrial machine with tremendous suction.

It was about time we had a car and one day we were all out driving and we passed a yellow Nash Ambassador for sale, so we stopped to take a look. It was a lovely car, huge inside with all leather couch seats front and back. Six people could sit in the back. It had a huge trunk. It was a 1951 model and had Hydra-Matic automatic transmission. I couldn't resist and with Jenny's prompting I bought it. It also had an extra body with it.

Carole began working on an early Mac, producing computer drawings by going into the "Fatbits" facility and working at pixel level. Using the alias "Lena Fatbitz", she made large wall sized drawings which were shown at a gallery in Sacramento

There are thousands of bicycles in Davis, a bit like Amsterdam. Carole got a bike from Bob's girlfriend, Sandy, that she just kept in the garage and never rode. It was a vintage pink Schwinn. I got a bike as well and we loved riding around together. A favourite route was alongside Putah Creek. Eventually they were both stolen and we never replaced them.

Sometime in 1983, Carole and Heidi and I, as part of Jenny's entourage, were invited to Marilyn Ferguson's wedding to Ray Gottlieb. Marilyn was a leading light in the New Age movement and was a big supporter of Jenny. She had published the Brain Mind Bulletin in Los Angeles, had written the best seller, "The Aquarian Conspiracy" and was a founder member of the Association of Humanistic Psychology. I recall phoning her to ask for a quote for a Jenny advertising flyer we were doing. She said that Jenny was one of the best teachers she had ever met.

We were not invited to the wedding itself but to the party and on the day before a message came asking us to pick up the wedding cake for her and take it to the party with us. When we arrived at the cake shop we were asked to pay for it, and, as usual, it was me that reluctantly did.

The party was fine and it was a bit awkward to ask for the money there and then, and it took several weeks and phone calls before I was finally reimbursed. Marilyn was a celebrity, a spiritual heavyweight with friends like Ram Dass, Al Gore and Ted Turner but even so I needed the money and I had to be robust.

In the autumn of 1983, Jenny and Russell decided to come and live with us in Davis and obviously we needed a bigger place to rent and we found a large detached house in a very posh area called El Macero, just outside Davis. We moved Heidi to the Pioneer school by the local golf course. All the other parents had shiny new cars but we would drop her off in the Nash. We called it, "Nasher". The mothers were wealthy and very straight and wore clothes that matched their status in the community. Not like us of course, we had no status.

The house had a drive at the front with a detached garage. There was a large hall with a lounge area to the left with a huge fireplace. Next left was a bedroom with an en suite. To the right was a modern kitchen then a sunken living area with French doors to the grassed back yard. Further right were three bedrooms, a utility room and a bathroom. We had the right wing, and Jenny and Russell the left wing. I began to organise groups for Jenny and got an extensive mailing list together and people she already knew travelled to El Macero to take part.

A millionaire friend of Marilyn called Rinaldo Brutoco was introduced to Jenny. He has written many books on the theme of spirituality and integrity in business. He lent us one of the early Macs and I began working on a book of Nine quotes which became known as the Silver Book. I had access to some of the transcripts which were marked red for private, and green for public.

I am glad to say I kept many of the greens as most of the archive has now been lost or destroyed. Our friend David Anderson had some which he shared with me. I regret not taking some of the reds as well. Bob Leach printed the book for us. I think there were a hundred copies made. My favourite quote was the Nine's answer to being asked,

"Which came first the chicken or the egg?

Their immediate response was,

"Nothing to do with the chicken or egg, but the stopping of flow for a moment called time and in this span reality is produced. This makes time and speed words describing the stopping of flow, and the latter how fast you can make the stop last."

It was a fertile period. We also produced a comic strip which Carole illustrated called "The Adventures of Chaotica". It contained lines like "Where does almost live... Down Practic Alley", and "How do I handle the world? Take a very firm grip on it, then take your gloves off."

We went to a party at the Brutoco mansion. Out back, there was what I can only describe as a temple with an altar, and murals of a spiritual nature. There were photographs of the guru Sai Baba in alcoves. He had millions of followers and miraculously produced sacred ash from his hand called "Vibhuti". It was supposed to have healing qualities and, like most of the gurus of the time, he was a controversial figure.

I had the Nash worked on by a friend called Carson who swapped the bodies as the spare was in better condition. I kept the carpet cleaner in the trunk and began to branch out for myself on the side. Sorry Donna, but needs must. I advertised in our local area and began to get work both for carpet and window cleaning. Heidi came with me sometimes. People there didn't have their windows cleaned regularly but usually twice a year both in and out. Anyway, it meant we had a bit more money.

It was then that I found a friend that I still have to this day. I was in Donna's house one hot afternoon and was just wandering around. It was a large rambling house, and I walked into one of the back rooms and I saw what looked like a guitar, wrapped in a blanket, leaning against the wall. I shouted through to Donna, "Hey Donna is this a guitar here?" and she shouted back that it was and to take a look. I unwrapped it and saw it was a small bodied Martin acoustic. It was out of tune, of course, but had all its strings. I tuned it up and strummed it. It was beautiful, rich tone, low action, easy to play. I had to own it. I asked her why she had a guitar when she didn't play.

She told me that it had belonged to her ex husband in New York. He had been a drug dealer and someone didn't pay him and they, amongst other things, had taken this guitar off him. When they were divorced she had brought the guitar with her to California to annoy him. Years later, when I looked up the serial number, 188631, I found out it is a 1963 Martin 0018. Donna agreed to sell it to me for maybe $200; I can't remember the exact amount. I couldn't afford it, so she kindly agreed to take it out of my wages every week. I still play it now and anyone who plays guitar always wants a go on it. It proudly wears the dings and scars of experience and has matured beautifully.

Donna also turned me on to the work of Stanley Kelleman, the Somatic--Emotional teacher. His current book was called "Your Body Speaks Its Mind". He was in the lineage of Wilhelm Reich and the Bioenergetics guy Alexander Lowen. It was another angle to learn.

At Christmas, JZ and Freddy came to stay and Freddy brought a huge Christmas tree. We had to trim the top to fit it in the house. Perry Carrison and his friend Tom, who they always referred to as "The Murderer", also came to visit.

Perry came with us all to a Nine session with Richard Hoagland. He was a conspiracy theorist and had become very involved with the photographs taken of Mars by NASA supposedly showing a face and some pyramids. He wrote several books proposing civilisations on Mars and other planets. NASA had always said it was an optical illusion. Anyway, he wanted confirmation from the Nine which I think they did not give him. He was very interested in why he had been chosen to make this discovery.

At that Christmas I also did one of the funniest business scams. There was a must-have Christmas toy called "Cabbage

Patch Kids". Parents were desperate to buy them for their children. It was a craze that had gone global after Coleco, the toy firm, had bought the rights. People were queuing for hours and fights were breaking out. The kids and parents in El Macero were no different. It was getting impossible to buy one.

I contacted my Mum in England and after a bit of research she told me they were not really that popular there yet and they could get me as many as I wanted. We sold a few dozen at triple the price they cost us, including the shipping. The snooty mums at Heidi's school bought most of them. Heidi got three. We had a very good Christmas.

Every spring there is a three day annual event in Davis called "The Whole Earth Festival". It was started as a small arts project in 1969 by Jose Arguello. Now it draws thousands of people. I applied to rent a space to read Tarot and was accepted. I had been studying tarot symbols and history and learned with Jenny. We found a table which Carole painted with mystic signs and I set up. I was really busy. Most of the time I was tripping on LSD, only half a tab though. The punters seemed to get a lot from my readings and I often had a queue.

There were craft stalls, alternative stuff of all kinds, an agricultural show, and music. The M.C. was Wavy Gravy. He was a hippy, peace activist clown. I believe he was given his name by B.B. King. The event was monitored by volunteers called the "Karma Patrol". We also sang on the big stage. We named ourselves "The Met", and sang our songs. I had written some material with Jenny.

On the fourth of July we went to a fireworks display in Davis. In the evening we took acid. It was a warm, balmy evening under a starry, cloudless sky. Later we went to Shannon's and sat out in the back yard. I sat in a carved wooden chair with a high back and had the best trip.

The chair took off and flew up into the sky, after a while it came down again and landed inside a huge slightly pink/beige dome. We landed in the centre on a dais. I could barely see the walls of the dome as it was so huge. The air was shimmering with light. I could see a few people in the distance but I could not make out what they were doing.

Suddenly a figure appeared in front of me. It was a woman. She must have been seven feet tall. She had golden skin and golden eyes. She was wrapped in a long golden cloak and the collar of her garment was a sunburst behind her head. She wore a golden pyramid hat made of thousands of tiny gold bricks. She pointed at me and her hand was golden with long golden nails. I swallowed. Still pointing she said, "Now wake up to this!" It was a command. My body jerked forward and my eyes closed then opened. She said it again and again, and my body jerked every time. It was like being jump started.

I don't know how much time passed but later I woke up back in the garden and fell into a deep, dreamless sleep. I have no doubt she was real. I could say, "As real as me", but she was probably more real, and certainly more powerful. I got that waking up is not a once only affair but an ongoing moment by moment process, easily forgotten. It became obvious to me that anything I have ever learned has come from outside my Geoffreyness and the inertia of usual me has to be breached over and over again.

Jenny discovered she was pregnant with Sullivan and she and Russell decided to get married but not in Davis. Betty Fuller offered her home in Tiburon on Belvedere Avenue and the marriage took place there on February 13th 1984. It was a fantastic house built like a little castle and set in grounds overlooking San Francisco Bay.

I played guitar and sang "Going to the Chapel" with Romily Grau, Kai's girlfriend. Heidi was bridesmaid and Carole was matron of honour. JZ and Freddy came as well as Dick Price who spent most of the time playing with balloons with Heidi.

In the meantime, we had become friendly with the owner of JoJo's pizza restaurant around the corner and we somehow got the job of making what he called closed pizzas for his stand at the upcoming blues festival in Sacramento. This involved the whole family working at night after he closed. We would work through the night. The pizzas we made were then frozen. We all had our own job to do. Mine was baking the pizzas in the big wood fired stove. I learned how to use a pizza peel after burning my hands several times.

Jenny chopped vegetables; she had to sit down at the counter as she was getting quite big. Carole made the pizzas up and did a lot of Jenny's work as well. I think Russell helped make up the pizzas and put the finished ones in boxes ready to be frozen. We had to make hundreds and we made good money as it took us a few weeks to do.

We also supplied JoJo with scotch eggs for a while, which we talked him into trying. We cooked these at home until the day when Russell took a tray of them out of the oven and put it on the floor in and melted the lino. We had to leave El Macero soon after as we couldn't afford the rent anymore and Carole spent hours painting the burn with matching colours to hide it from the landlord. We did owe back-rent and Russell and I worked it off by doing painting jobs for him.

I got back into playing rugby again. There was a big interest in rugby union and several leagues. Many of the US players had played American football and there were lots of expats from Australia and New Zealand. Russell was a really good fullback and we joined a club in Davis. We began training and I can still remember the feeling of the first tackle. I was in the seconds and played quite a few games. I forgot my shorts once but no-one would lend me a pair as they were all paranoid about AIDS. The players were all characters, and the chief one was nicknamed "The Demon". He was a hard drinking, no nonsense guy. I was surprised when I found out he was a vet.

Carole was making work as usual and she got a piece called "Madame Motivation" into a competition at the Crocker Kingsley Art Museum in Sacramento. She also got a sculpture of Heidi, called "Sasha" into a competition at the Laguna Beach Museum of Modern Art. It was recently resold online.

We visited Esalen quite a few times as well. The first time we drove there in the Nash down Highway One, a narrow cliff edge road that stretches from San Francisco to Los Angele, it seemed like we would never get there but eventually we got to the Big Sur coast and finally saw the wooden sign "Esalen Institute by Reservation Only", and pulled in. We were stopped at the gate but Jenny had left word to let us in. We pulled over to the left and parked by Fritz Perls' house. It had a balcony overlooking the Pacific where there was a massage table. Ida Rolf is supposed to have massaged Fritz there.

Jenny was running a group there that evening and around fifty people turned up. Afterwards we had something to eat and our first hot tub, then Trevor found Carole and me a spare cabin to sleep in, and Heidi slept in Fritz's bedroom.

Clothes were optional but people were always dressed in the dining area. At first being naked and seeing others naked was quite confronting. My inner talk went into overdrive, comparing and contrasting but eventually it calmed down. I have to say an erotic element always remains although it gets less intense. There was also a big outdoor pool where it seemed to me all the especially beautiful looking people hung out and I knew I wasn't in that club. Even then, they were all eating vegan organic food, drinking wheatgrass and recycling. I just loved it there. I know some people found it difficult and everyone will have a different story to tell.

Sometimes we stayed at South Coast which was a property just up the road. It also had a swimming pool and a sauna. I remember happy, sunny days swimming naked in the pool with Carole and Heids and JZ and Freddy.

The Nash did not have air conditioning and on one trip to Esalen it was so hot we would stop in every town, go to the local supermarket and stand by the fridges to cool down. Highway 1 was often closed by landslides and once we had to make a detour south to San Luis Obispo to come back north again. We stopped for gas and the garage guy told us that the highway was out from this side as well. I rang the number I had for Esalen. J.Z. answered and I asked her what to do. I told her the highway was out. She said it wasn't. I said that was what the garage guy had said and she asked me if I would rather believe her or the garage guy. We drove up the highway and it was open of course.

We spent time with Dick Price, who ran Esalen. He was a small, wiry man and had a wonderful energy about him, intense and laid-back at the same time. I had been writing songs and we sang some for him. He called Heidi "Little Nine". She would sit in on many of the groups and would be an "Alter Ego" for the participants by sitting on a person's knee and speaking as them.

We met Will Schutz at a party in someone's house near San Francisco. I think it may have been JZ's birthday. It was a barbecue in the back yard. JZ and Will sat side by side like Queen and King. I don't recall him standing. He was a bald, stocky man. I was too nervous of him to have a conversation or even say hello.

I was told a story about the rivalry between Will and Fritz Perls. One evening, they were both in the grounds of Esalen near the fire. Fritz had his followers near him and so did Will. They were debating some point about therapy and it got heated until they were shouting at each other. They were both passionate men and into being real. Then they began to bark like dogs and a growling Fritz tried to bite Will. They had to be pulled apart.

We couldn't afford the rent anymore in El Macero so we decided to live separately again. Carole, Heidi and I rented a small apartment for the summer at Heritage House on Sycamore. It was a very large student complex with a swimming pool. Most of the students had gone home for the summer. Jenny and Russell rented a little duplex house with a back garden full of tall bamboo. We grew marijuana plants hidden in the foliage. Jenny was pregnant and very fed up. It was very hot and she would sit in front of a large block of ice with an electric fan trying to keep cool. They moved back to the Watsonville area and Sullivan was born there in July 1984.

Heidi joined the school softball team. They played in the rookies' league. We have a picture of her posing with the other girls. They wore red baseball caps, a red shirt and white shorts. Their sponsors were Efstratis and Corbett who were parents. I loved watching her play. If a girl missed the ball, but it wasn't a strike, you had to call out, "Good eye, good eye" for encouragement as if they had done it on purpose. We did that a lot!

Towards the end of the summer we had moved again. We rented two bedrooms in Laurie's house on Lafayette. She was a student vet. She had two dogs; the older one was called "Hooker", who often weed on the floor, and the younger black one was called Nicholas. The first thing I did was to clean the carpets with Donna's machine.

We moved the four marijuana plants to her garden at the back of the house under cover of darkness, in the back of the Nash. The buds were nice and sparkly by now, but the night before I had decided to harvest them someone broke in and stole them except for the smallest one. I had heard the dogs barking in the night but took no notice. I never found out who took them. I could hardly complain to the police.

Carole began cutting hair and managed to get quite a few clients. She set up a salon in the house. We acquired a large mirror and set light bulbs around it like an actor's dressing room. She created radical haircuts well ahead of her time and also decorated their nails, in the way girls have them now, with her own designs.

Our time at Laurie's ended and we rented a place from Linda Frieze. It was one of my favourite houses. It was an old converted barn, half was living quarters and half studio. It was situated over the railroad tracks and down a long dirt road into the corn fields. Several huge fig trees grew at the front and I got sick by eating too many, but really fresh figs are amazing. As many houses did, it had orange trees at the front which fruited in December.

Linda's front door opened into a country style kitchen and then into a large living area, with an exposed wooden floor. There were two bedrooms on the right with old fashioned beds and a bathroom on the left. Another door on the left led into the studio with a high roof up to the barn's rafters. I was still working at Miller Maintenance with Donna, but in the afternoons we stayed in bed and watched black and white reruns of "The Honeymooners", the Jackie Gleason show, and the sitcom "Leave It To Beaver" on TV.

One weekend, we visited Kai's for a big party and barbecue and caught giardia, a stomach parasite from the water. When we got home we started to be ill but didn't know why. We felt sick and had upset stomachs but then it went away, re-appeared, and then seemingly went away again. Stupidly, we just left it and did nothing.

I have discovered how connected I feel to the people I have been writing about. They are all alive in me. In a way they are me. They speak through me. They experience the world through me, and it ripples out. All the people they knew, and all the people known to them, they too speak and live through me. Everyone who ever lived still lives through each one of us. I am but a moment in an unbroken line, a bird perched on a twig of a strange tree whose roots stretch back millennia. I have just added my few years of experience.

What a wonder to be able to bud, fruit, ripen and decay, to make an appearance on this stage. Out of all the possibilities, it was you and me who made it here as human beings. We won the race to be here. Through us, life is living this thing we call life until it is passed to the next baton holders and then we will live on through them. But as every generation discovers, life is a struggle not only physically but also in labouring under the weight of the culture in which we find ourselves, the lure of temporary pleasures and the degree of dissatisfaction that we are required to experience to keep us consuming more and more as we try to hide in the conceptual world, ignore what we are doing to each other, and squander our birthright.

Chapter Fifteen

Aptos and Watsonville

Although we were settled in Davis and had an income, with Jenny and Russell's promptings we decided to move closer to Esalen and to Kai's where they were now living, so we moved again. It was to a house, owned by a relative of Kai's, in Aptos, a little town just off highway one, south of Santa Cruz. We hired a U-Hall truck, loaded up the Nash and headed south on the freeway. It took us all day and when we arrived in the late afternoon we were hot and really tired. We had found the main road, Valencia, but the house was on Hayward off the road and down into the woods. You could see houses dotted around randomly amongst the redwoods and eucalyptus. All of them were wooden and some were painted.

The house that we were headed to, number 150, was painted red, but it was peeling in many places, and although it was around 35 degrees up on the main road, down in the woods it was much cooler in the shade of the tree canopy, even so, the rays of the sun angled through here and there, catching the edges of the leaves, and lighting the ground in white pools of light.

I sighed as I saw the house and the number and realised this was our destination. I knew, by looking, that it was derelict, but I didn't want to admit this to myself. It had been a pretty house, at some point in the past, in a lovely location. A tall brick chimney grew up one wall. It was on three floors set in the centre of a little valley, and part of the back stood on stilts over a little creek. I later found it was called Trout Creek. The road on the other side of the little valley was Trout Gulch Road. Someone had erected a large wooden screen in the trees on the other side, for projecting movies onto.

I had never seen the house before and had taken it on trust that it would be ok, but my sense was that it was not. I pulled up and got out and Carole and Heidi pulled up in the Nash too. We were all silent after our long drive. This was meant to be a new start. We looked at the house and then at each other. We had little money and going back to Davis was not an option.

"Let's go in" I said, rubbing my hands together and trying to sound positive, but I knew I wasn't fooling them. I got the key out of my pocket and unlocked the door. It creaked as it opened. Inside it was worse than I feared. It had been vandalised and there was broken bits of stuff scattered on the floor. There were empty beer cans strewn everywhere and someone had written in bright red paint aerosol across the walls. I tried the light switch - nothing. I tried the tap in the sink in the kitchen and the shower room, and they both worked. We had cold water but no way of heating it, no gas and no electricity, but a phone landline that worked. I looked at the toilet, it was filthy and it stank. I flushed it and it flushed. I flushed it again several times.

"The windows are all broken," said Carole, "and the carpet is filthy."

"Where's my room?" said Heidi, "I'm not sleeping on my own here!"

There was no arguing with that, none of us wanted to sleep on our own, none of us wanted to sleep there at all.

"Is this what we have come to?" I thought, "Let's look downstairs" I said, trying to appear cheerful and positive.

We all walked down the stairs to the second floor. It was a mess too. We didn't even dare to go down to the third floor.

But as we had nowhere else to go, and little money, we reluctantly unloaded our belongings off the U-Haul. By then, it was getting dark. What to do for dinner? We went to a local cafe and had potato skins and cheese. I had coffee, Carole tea, and Heidi a coke. We dragged out the time to go home but eventually we could put it off no longer.

We left the cafe, got in the Nash and drove the ten minutes it took back to the house. It was a pretty drive, the sun going down and shining the air red through the trees. The air was still warm and smelled of eucalyptus. Down the track we drove and finally disembarked.

That night, we all slept together on our California King Size mattress. We were still feeling unwell, and when I spoke to Kai the next morning to tell her we had arrived, she confirmed that they all had giardia and were taking medication. I had no choice.

I went to the local doctors' surgery and told them we had giardia and we didn't need a test because our friends had it and they agreed to sell me the necessary medication, more or less wiping out our money. Out of our 80 dollars, 60 went on medication and 20 on dinner.

Gradually, bit by bit, by doing odd jobs, we repaired the house. We put in new windows, cleaned the carpet, painted over graffiti, bleached and re-bleached the toilet. As there was no electricity, we bought oil lamps from a yard sale and someone lent us an old fashioned wooden ice box that you put a block of ice in at the bottom. It worked quite well.

At first we cooked in the open fireplace with wood we had collected, but later we acquired a camping stove and felt quite posh. Heidi went to the local school, no questions asked. It was the E.A. Hall Middle School, 210 Brewington Street, Watsonville. The school district was Pajoro Valley. She was picked up every day, at the top of the track near the mailboxes, by the yellow school bus. We settled in but we were living day to day.

We were relying on odd jobs for the locals so I decided to get some decent money in by going up to Davis and doing some Tarot readings. I contacted Shannon who said I could stay with her and she and Donna would book me sessions. I travelled up by Greyhound. I had just enough money for the fare and when I got to Davis I had to walk to Shannon's from the bus station. I had a shower when I got there, a luxury we did not have in Aptos. They had booked me a lot of sessions and I really enjoyed myself.

Shannon lent me her bike and I cycled around Davis to my appointments. I made over three hundred dollars, enough for my ticket back and plenty left over. Shannon was very hospitable to me.

When I arrived back, Russell picked me up in the Nash. He said he had news for me. When we got to Aptos, I found that we now had lodgers. Sherry Kluge and her daughter Shawna, who was about the same age as Heidi, had moved into the second floor of the house. Sherry's mum was Anita Storey, who had been Marilyn Ferguson's secretary in L.A., and had worked with her on her book, "The Aquarian Conspiracy".

Sherry was broke and couldn't afford to pay us rent. A few weeks later Kai's relative came to see us and told us we had to move out. I think he wanted to develop it. I told him we had nowhere else to go, and he left us alone after that.

Jenny was in touch with the media mogul Ted Turner and did some Nine sessions with him. He was writing a book and had given it to Jenny to look at. We went to a party around this time and met Ted Turner's girlfriend, J.J. Ebaugh. She had a DeLorean car and Heids enjoyed sitting in it.

It was a dual life again, meeting rich people and having little money ourselves. We still had no regular work and I did various odd jobs. I did french polishing for a day. I had no money to buy some food to take with me for lunch and the man made me a cheese burrito. I think he was sorry for me.

I was hired to dig a new toilet pit at Kai's. They did have a flush toilet but also had a hand-made wooden cubicle in the fields. It was beautifully carved and had a split door, so when you sat there you could look out over the Redwood Mountains and see the Pacific in the distance. A new pit was dug every few years. The depth had to be twice my height and my outstretched arms wide. It took me two days to dig it. As I got deeper I could almost hear distant singing in Hebrew and I realised later it had been Yom Kippur, the Day of Atonement. My body tingled with a strange feeling. The next day the wooden building was lifted up and moved to its new location.

Then Russell and I worked on the cherry tree house. The hole in the roof, through which the tree grew, had to be resealed every year as the tree got bigger. The silliest job I ever got was with Russell. We had to remove the branches of a tree overhanging a six person hot tub at a house in Santa Cruz. We hired a chain saw. Russell was up in the tree cutting away and one of the big branches fell on the full hot tub smashing it. The water flooded the garden. The owners quite rightly refused to pay us. They claimed on their house insurance as we had none.

I found a job as a Santa Claus which was advertised in the local free paper "Good Times". I rang up and got an interview the next day in Capitola nearby. When I arrived at the address, a small office block by the Pacific, I was met by Harvey Cohen, a little Jewish guy. He was a bit of a hustler and owned a PR advertising agency. He gave me the job as soon as he heard my English accent. There was no vetting, imagine that now.

The location was in a new shopping mall in Santa Cruz and I went there with Harvey to check it out. It was a grotto on the second floor decorated by a very cool shop in Santa Cruz called Lilly Wong. There was a big Christmas tree covered in glitter, artificial snow on the floor and boxes of presents all piled up. The deal was that a child would have their photo taken with me and then return the next day to collect the print. This was years before digital photography or smart phones. I had a really great Santa suit and two months paid work, heaven. I would dress up as Santa and then drive up the highway to Santa Cruz in the Nash. I was honked and waved at all the way. Once the Nash broke down on the highway and Santa got a lift instantly. The family who picked me up were so excited to have a real live Santa in the car with them.

Harvey had decided that he would be my elf helper and dressed in a green jacket, red trousers, red pointy shoes, and a little green hat. He took the pictures and I would give the child a candy cane. A Jewish Santa with a Jewish elf.

The kids were lovely. They were at an age when they really believed and would whisper in my ear. Often it was not about what they wanted for Christmas but questions about what it was like at the North Pole, or where Rudolph lived. Sometimes, energised by their faith, I felt like I was channelling Santa.

At that time, the drug ecstasy or MDMA had become very popular on the west coast. It was also being used therapeutically with terminally ill patients. I remember seeing a Phil Donahue TV show, a debate about the efficacy of MDMA between therapists and representatives of the FBI. The audience was comprised of ill people who had used it and found it really helpful in facing up to their situation but it was still made illegal in July 1985.

We had been taking it for fun as Jenny knew a researcher at the University of California at Berkeley who was making it. It came as a yellow powder and we mixed it into coffee. I think it was different from the ecstasy sold later in England that ravers would use and dance on all night. We never got that weird jaw thing. For me it was just being in very clear space, extremely mellow, and "all loved up" as they say.

Anyway, Harvey was a big ecstasy fan. He had given me the key to the grotto and I would get there first and open up. One morning he was really late. I waited and waited but a mother arrived with her little girl to have her picture taken. I explained the situation and she left her daughter with me and went off shopping.

Suddenly Harvey appeared in his pixie costume, obviously out of it. He grabbed the little girl, and shouting "Ho, Ho, Ho," rolled over and over with her in the polystyrene snow. I jumped up, rescued the girl and put her on the Santa seat. She was more surprised than anything else. I pointed at him and shouted, "Harvey, go home!" He didn't argue, and with head bowed, my elf slowly and shamefully left the grotto. I sacked my boss. I took the girl on my knee and we chatted for a while. The mum came back and we improvised by her taking the photo as I realised the camera was already set up.

The next day he apologised to me. He was married but having an affair, and he and his girlfriend had taken ecstasy, driven up to San Francisco and gone on a helicopter ride around the bay. They had been up all night.

He hired me as Santa for other jobs. There was a Santa movie out and we went to the cinema in Santa Cruz and handed out leaflets advertising the grotto to the people as they left. He also shot a movie of me as Santa for his son who lived with his ex wife in another state. He wrote a script and we went to the beach and I acted the little play. I was roasting on the beach in my Santa outfit but he paid me well.

Carole and I found a job working on the next mountain to Kai's for Elizabeth Jarbo. She was an older woman whose husband, Owen, had dementia. They had money so she did not want to put him in a home and paid for twenty four hour care for him. They lived in a log house in a clearing at the top of a long track. There were wooden stairs up to a stoop at the front. It was a twelve hour shift and she paid us cash and provided all meals. It was not a difficult job.

There were little tasks to do as well. If you were the morning shift you had to get the wood burner going which provided heat for the stove. Elizabeth gave me other jobs too, like digging a trench for electrical cables, which took me a week to do. I also dug a new cess pit for her. I had quite a reputation as a cess pit digger.

In January 1986, the winter rains were really bad in Aptos and several houses were washed away in the mountains. All the locals pitched in and helped each other. The authorities came to our locale and advised everyone in the woods to move out for a few days for safety. We had already experienced an earth quake there. It was in the middle of the night and the house began to shake. We all got up. The floor felt like it was rolling and the plates in the cupboards were rattling. Some drawers opened and cutlery flew out. We stood outside in our pajamas for a while. We could see some of our neighbours in the trees doing the same. After a while we all went back to bed. It was California and there were earthquakes.

We decided to go into the local shelter which was run by the Red Cross. We only lasted two nights there. We slept on cots in a big dormitory with people coughing and farting and babies crying. We couldn't sleep so we went back home.

Jenny and Russell had been living at Kai's and it was time for them to leave and although it had been romantic living in the woods in Aptos it was time to get back into the modern world. So we rented a house with them and Sullivan, their new baby, in Watsonville on East Beach Street opposite the high school. We were near crossroads and I would watch the young Chicanos in their low rider cars bouncing up and down at the traffic lights. Sherry and Shawna stayed in Aptos.

Our new abode was a modern wooden detached house with a drive up the side. Jenny and Russell had the upstairs and we had the downstairs. What a relief it was to have electricity again and to have a shower whenever I wanted.

We were still chronically short of money. One day I was walking in town with Heidi when a homeless man came up to me begging money. I only had five dollars left but I gave it to him. I knew I may never have this chance again. It was as if a huge weight had been lifted off me.

One night I was woken by the phone ringing. It was Sherry who was still living in the condemned house in Aptos. She begged me for help. She said she was in Capitola police station and had been arrested for non payment of traffic fines that had caught up with her from L.A. She needed two hundred dollars to be released. Since I had given my last five dollars away, Carole and I had been able to save up some money.

I told her not to worry, metaphorically donned my knight in shining armour costume and rushed out to the Nash. I left a note for Carole, which I still have, explaining where I had gone. I got in the Nash and on the steering wheel was a piece of paper saying "Ha-ha, got you". I was livid. I could hardly speak. What made it worse for my self-importance was that everybody thought it was great fun and laughed at me. It was a great lesson.

Even though my intentions were good I was caught in my default rescue routine. My view of myself and how I expected others to treat me given my magnanimous generosity was severely shaken.

Once again our home was open house for anyone who was in some kind of crisis or who had been to Esalen and needed support. It was like being in a group therapy every day. Sometimes our visitors paid to live with us, sometimes they didn't. It got fraught between us all and we began to argue. Jenny had a new TV and as we didn't have one, I decided to buy her old one. It was in our bedroom but I hadn't given her the cash yet. Carole was doing an overnight shift at the Jarbos and I woke up early. It was July 1986 and I found the Wimbledon men's final on the TV, made myself a coffee and settled down to watch it. It was Becker against Lendl. Sullivan appeared at the door. He said that his mummy had sent him down to watch cartoons on the TV. I said that he couldn't as I was watching something. He went out then re-appeared and we had the same conversation. Off he went and this time, Jenny appeared. We had a shouting match and struggled with the TV. I gave in and she took the TV upstairs. We didn't speak for days.

The next incident was a fight between Carole and Jenny in the kitchen. It ended with Jenny pushing Carole backwards through a window which broke. Carole hadn't fought back because Jenny was pregnant again. Although we had some really wonderful times together, and had laughed so much, the bad times were getting bigger and longer.

JZ visited us and stayed for a few days and tried to lift our spirits. I remember eating half-a-chicken burritos together but even she could not mend the relationship. I was just getting fed up of being poor.

We had a friend called Ben, not his real name, who was a very big cannabis wholesaler. We had met him when he bought Carole's ceramic sculpture, "Madame Motivation". He approached Russell and asked if we could help him out. The FBI had mounted a sting operation against some medium level dope dealers who were anxious to move up the ladder. The undercover agents had told these two guys that a very big shipment was arriving somewhere by sea but that it would cost over a million dollars. The dealers did not have that kind of money so the undercover agents said that they could lend them the money and after lots of negotiations it was all agreed.

The money was lent and when the two dealers turned up to collect their merchandise they were busted. Ben was a very careful man and when he heard about this he decided to just shut up shop for a while. He was concerned that the busted guys might have his phone number recorded somewhere and he wanted to take no chances.

He had several houses rented in other people's names and several cars. The plan was to move all the contents of the houses and the cars into storage, also rented in other people's names. It took us a few weeks to accomplish this. There was really nice stuff including vintage leather sofas and chairs and vintage rosewood furniture. There were also several very heavy safes. We moved the contents first in a hired van and then the safes. Last of all we moved the cars. He was very concerned about someone seeing the registration so we did it in a convoy of three vehicles, a rental car at the front, the hidden car second and a rental car at the rear.

When we were done he paid us in cash. I went straight to the local travel company and bought three air tickets to England. I thought we might never see that much money again.

After that, Jenny and I didn't speak much. We had a yard sale and sold most of our stuff and went to stay at Kai's. We slept in a tent in the blue sleeping bags we had brought over with us four years previously. I never saw Jenny again until years later on Skype when she was living in Byron Bay in Australia.

I had such mixed feelings about going. I had loved the adventure of being in California, the weather, the cities, the ocean, the scenery and the amazing people we met. I had loved Jenny and Russell and being part of Jenny's crazy trip. It had all set me up for a long and successful career as a psychotherapist, but enough was enough.

I had never laughed so much or felt so low. I had looked at myself and my attachment to my little Geoffrey ways and sometimes not liked what I saw. I had found a spiritual resilience of my own as well as knowing that I could survive from my own inner strength with the love of Carole and Heidi. I had loved Jenny and felt her love. I know many people who met her through Esalen who felt they had an extra special relationship with her. However, I can say we were brother and sister, and in the time we lived together I saw her off-stage, behind the curtain, and sometimes it was not pretty. I also know some who experienced her as a malign influence in their lives, but I have no regrets. She changed my life and I have daily used and continue to use her ways and teachings in my work and in my life.

Through being around her and her direct no-compromise warrior attitude I had been able get the simplicity of being with "what is" and the very real fantasy of Geoffrey's stories about the world. I learned to see how I am caught in what Dion Fortune called the "Ring Pass-Not" and how my self-important draining attachment to me is what gives me the fantasy of being separate, me versus the world. I still miss her but I had to leave to find all this and more.

We left the Nash parked halfway up Kai's mountain, and Ben drove us to San Francisco airport. I had alerted my brother Paul and he agreed to pick us up at Heathrow. I asked him not to tell Mum and Dad. The plane landed and we got off into the cold and onto a shuttle train to the terminal and the recorded very

English voice told us what we could and could not do. We laughed. It was good to see Paul and he drove us up to Southport and it was still there. I walked up the steps at Saunders Street and rang the bell. Dad answered the door and I hugged him, then I hugged Mum. Financially, it had cost us everything, we only had fifty dollars left, but even though the price of the adventure was worth it, it was good to be home.

Carole and Me, Southport, 1968

Mum, 1940s

Dad 1940s

Grandma Celia, 1920s

Grandpa David and Grandma Celia, 1920s

Grandpa David, First World War

Grandpa Gustav, First World War

Grandma Paula and Grandpa Gustav, 1920s

Grandma Elsa, 1920s

Dad and Uncle Oskar, 1930s

Windmüller Family Home, Rodenberg, 1920s
Dad and Elsa in the doorway

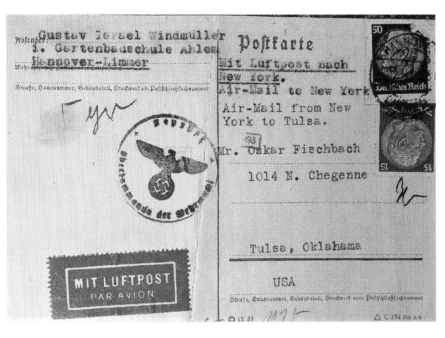

Gustav and Elsa's Plea to USA, 1941 (page 39)

Great Grandma Susanna, 1930s

Great Aunt Selma, 1930s

Great Grandpa Eli holding Mum and Vivi 1925

Great, Great Grandma Mera with her four sons, c1900

Dad's Release from Sachsenhausen-Oranienburg Concentration Camp,
January 1939

Dad's Exemption from Internment, N. Ireland, October 1939

Home Office No. V.19321.

Certificate No. DZ 3103

Certificate of Naturalization granted to a woman
who was at birth a British subject and is married to a subject
of a State at war with His Majesty

Whereas   Syrilla Rose Windham

who was at birth a British subject and is the wife of an alien who is a subject of a State at war with His Majesty, has made a declaration that she desires to resume British nationality and has applied to one of His Majesty's Principal Secretaries of State for a Certificate of Naturalization alleging with respect to herself the particulars set out below :

And whereas the Secretary of State is satisfied that it is desirable that the said

Syrilla Rose Windham

be permitted to resume British nationality and that such a certificate may properly be granted :

Now, therefore, in pursuance of the powers conferred on him by the said Act, the Secretary of State grants to the said

Syrilla Rose Windham

this Certificate of Naturalization, and declares that upon taking the Oath of Allegiance within the time and in the manner required by the regulations made in that behalf she shall, subject to the provisions of the said Act, be entitled to all political and other rights, powers and privileges, and be subject to all obligations, duties and liabilities to which a natural-born British subject is entitled or subject, and have to all intents and purposes the status of a natural-born British subject.

In witness whereof I have hereto subscribed my name this   6th   day of November, 1945.

Under Secretary of State.

HOME OFFICE,
LONDON.

PARTICULARS RELATING TO APPLICANT.

Full Name	Syrilla Rose WINDHAM.
Address	178, Elizabeth Street, Hightown, Manchester, 8.
Trade or Occupation	Schoolteacher.
Place and date of Birth	Salford, Lancashire. 24th November, 1925.
Nationality	German (by marriage).
Name of husband	Dennis WINDHAM otherwise Hans Jakob Israel WINDMÜLLER.
Names and nationality of parents	David and Celia SAMUELS. (British). (For Oath see overleaf)

Mum's Naturalisation from German back to British, November 1945

189

Our Butcher Shop in Hill St Southport, early 1960s
Mum and Paul at the front

Our Butcher Shop in Bold St Southport, 1970s

Insert Advert, 1970s

Packaging, 1970s

Me at the back with Stephen and Paul, 1957

Dad with Susan and baby Heidi, 1974

Dad, Grandma Celia, Me,
Mum, Paul, Grandpa David, Stephen, Vivi, 1956

Manny and Rita, Carole's Parents, 1930s

The Electrons, 1964

Marital Aids c 1980

The Nash in the drive at El Macero, Ca, 1983

Reading Tarot, Whole Earth Festival
Davis Ca, Spring 1983

Jenny O'Connor, c 1983

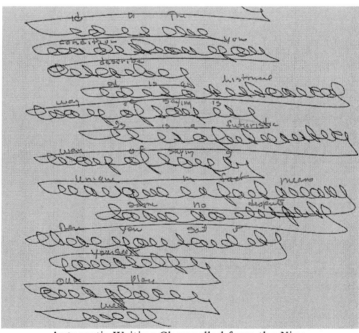

Automatic Writing Channelled from the Nine

Heidi, Davis Ca, 1983

Our house in Aptos Ca, 1985, Heidi at the front

Heidi and Santa, Santa Cruz Ca, 1985

Carole, Me and Madame Motivation,
Santa Cruz Ca, 1986

Acknowledgements

Carole and Heidi

Stephen, Paul and Susan

Ruth Bloom

Rachael Clyne (Hazel)

Phil Gray

John Taylor (Taz)

Alan Phillips

Geoffrey Samuel

Margaret Bilinsky Fischbach

Ruth Gutman

David Anderson

Shannon Sutherland

Shaun Hermel, Marlis Buchholz and the staff of the Israelitische Gartenbauschule Memorial, Ahlem, Hannover

Niedersächhsisches Landesarchiv, Hannover and Bückeberg

Gedenkstätte und Museum Sachsenhausen, Oranienburg

Koblenz Memorial Internet Site re Selma Grunewald

International Tracing Service, Bad Arolsen

National Archives, Kew

Army Personnel Support Division, Glasgow

heart & mind

Printed in Great Britain
by Amazon